# WHAT'S INSIDE PLANTS?

## ANITA GANERI

PETER BEDRICK BOOKS

NEW YORK

Published by
PETER BEDRICK BOOKS
2112 Broadway
New York, NY 10023

Published by agreement with
Macdonald Young Books Ltd, England.

Library of Congress Cataloging-in-
Publication Data

Ganeri, Anita, 1961–
What's inside plants? / Anita Ganeri.—1st
American ed.   p.   cm.—(What's Inside series)
Includes index.
ISBN 0-87226-397-5
1. Plants—Juvenile literature.
2. Botany—Anatomy—Juvenile literature.
3. Plant physiology—Juvenile literature.
[1. Plants. 2. Botany 3. Plant physiology.]
QK49.G36  1995
581—dc20
94–48545
CIP
AC

Commissioning Editor: Thomas Keegan
Designer: John Kelly
Editor: Nicky Barber
Illustrators: Brian Watson, David Cook
(Linden Artists); Maltings Partnership;
Kevin Maddison
Typesetters:
Goodfellow & Egan, Cambridge

First American edition 1995
Printed and bound in Hong Kong

Words in bold in the text can be found in
the Glossary on p.44

# Contents

What are plants made of?     8

Inside a leaf     10

Stomata – the inside story     12

Making food     14

Plant plumbing     16

What's in wood?     18

Bark in focus     20

Rooted to the spot     22

Journey through a flower     24

Beautiful colors     26

Autumn colors     28

Pollen precision     30

The secret of seeds     32

Growing up     34

Sensitive plants     36

Touch sensitive     38

Plants in water     40

Mystery fungi     42

Glossary     44

Index     45

# What are plants made of?

Plants, and all other living things, are made of microscopic building blocks called **cells**. All of a plant's vital chemical processes are carried out inside its cells. Some plants, such as *Chlamydomonas*, are single-celled. At the other end of the scale are the towering trees. They are made of millions upon millions of cells. In these larger plants, groups of cells work together to form tissues. Several different types of tissue work together as organs, such as leaves, roots or stems.

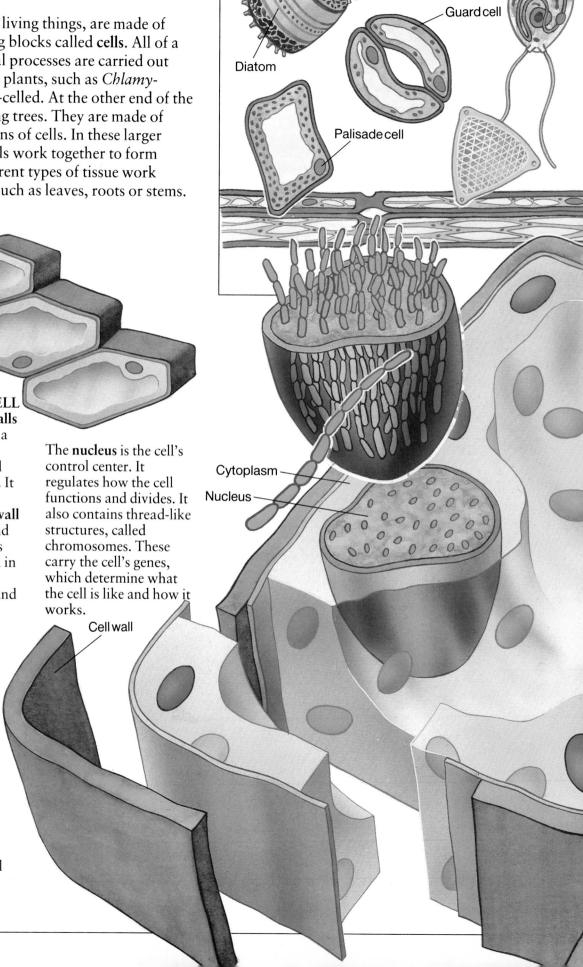

*Diatom*

*Chlamydomonas*

*Guard cell*

*Palisade cell*

*Cytoplasm*

*Nucleus*

*Cell wall*

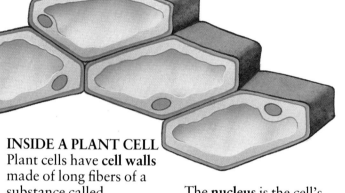

## INSIDE A PLANT CELL

Plant cells have **cell walls** made of long fibers of a substance called **cellulose**. The cell wall gives the cell its shape. It is easy to see under a microscope. The **cell wall** is the thin 'skin' around the whole cell. It keeps the contents of the cell in and allows certain substances to pass in and out of the cell.

The **cytoplasm** is 90 per cent water. It also contains grains of food and tiny structures called **organelles**. These are involved in the cell's chemical reactions, such as releasing energy and making food. They are vital for keeping the cell alive.

Plant cells are joined together along their cell walls. Fluids can pass through the cell walls from cell to cell.

The **nucleus** is the cell's control center. It regulates how the cell functions and divides. It also contains thread-like structures, called chromosomes. These carry the cell's genes, which determine what the cell is like and how it works.

## DIFFERENT CELLS
*Most plant cells follow the basic pattern shown in the diagram below, although some are specialized for doing particular jobs. Phloem cells carry food through a plant. The guard cells around a leaf's **stomata** are curved. **Palisade cells** are column-shaped cells. Chlamydomonas and diatoms are single-celled.*

Phloem cell

1. The parent cell is about to divide.

2. The nucleus divides into two and a dividing line, called the middle lamella, separates the two new cells.

3. A cellulose cell wall forms on either side of the middle lamella and the cell's cytoplasm divides in two.

4. One of the daughter cells develops a vacuole and grows bigger.

5. The other cell is able to divide again if necessary.

## GETTING GROWING
*Plants grow when their cells divide and increase in number. Cells also divide to replace and repair dead or worn-out cells. To divide, one 'parent' cell splits into two identical 'daughter' cells. One daughter usually becomes specialized to do a particular job. It cannot divide again. The other is able to divide and continue the plant's growth.*

Plastid

Vacuole

The living matter in the cell — the nucleus, cytoplasm and cell membrane — is known as the **protoplasm**.

**Vacuoles** are the large, fluid-filled spaces inside plant cells. The fluid they contain is called cell **sap**. It is made of dissolved sugars and minerals. It pushes against the cytoplasm and the cell wall to make the cell firm.

**Plastids** are one of the types of organelles found in a plant cell's cytoplasm. They include **chloroplasts** which contain the green **pigment**, **chlorophyll**, for making food (*see page 15*).

## CELL FACTS
*Diatoms are single-celled **algae** which live in salt or fresh water. They have cell walls made of a hard material called silica. When the plants die, their skeletons collect in their millions on the bottom of ponds or on the sea bed. Over time, some of these skeletons fossilize to form a substance called Fuller's earth. This is used in polish, paint and even in toothpaste.*

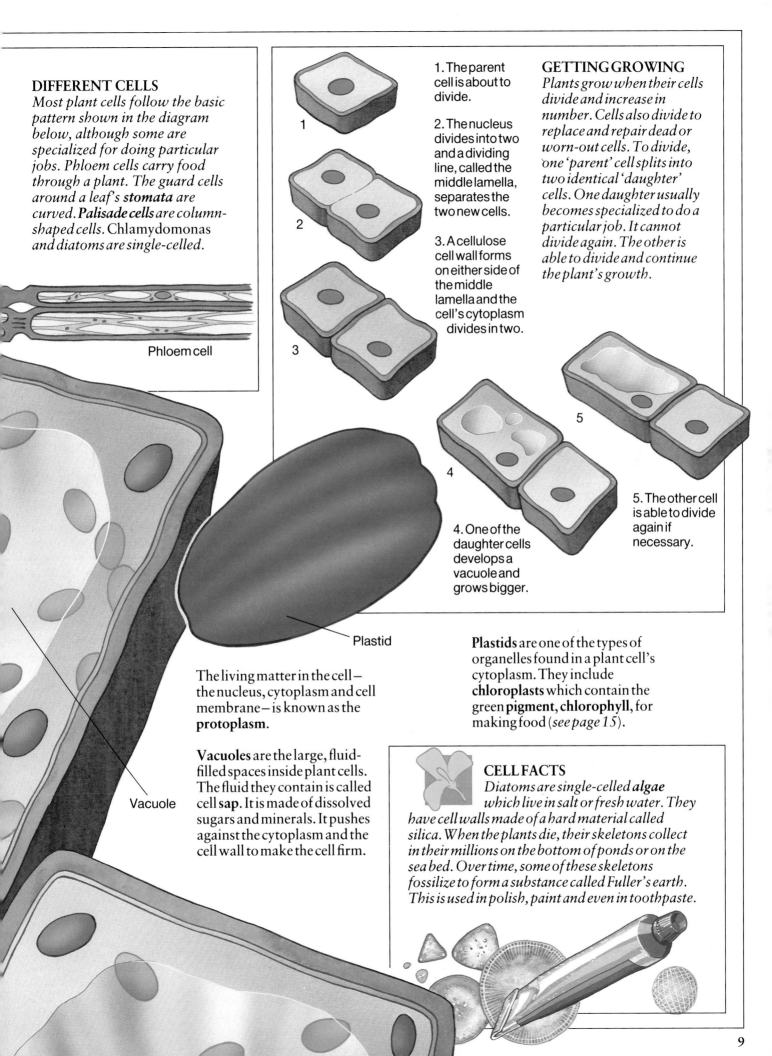

# Inside a leaf

Unlike animals, green plants can make their own food in a process called **photosynthesis**. In order for photosynthesis to occur a plant has to trap the sun's light. So the leaves of a plant are arranged on its stem to give the maximum possible surface area for catching sunlight. Gas also passes in and out of leaves to fuel photosynthesis and respiration and lose water through tiny holes in their leaves (**transpiration**).

## THE STRUCTURE OF A LEAF

The leaf blade, or lamina, is often broad for catching as much sunlight as possible. It is also thin so that gases and other substances can pass through it easily. The **epidermis** is a single layer of cells which grows like a skin over the leaf. The cells are usually transparent. Sunlight passes through them to the food-making chloroplasts below. The epidermis helps to keep the leaf in shape and protects the cells inside. It may be covered in a waxy cuticle which helps to waterproof the leaf.

The veins and midrib are part of the plant's **vascular tissue**, its transport system (*see pages 16–17*). They are made up of a network of fine tubes, some (**xylem**) carrying water into the leaf for photosynthesis and some (**phloem**) carrying food out. The veins also act as the leaf's skeleton, strengthening it and giving it shape.

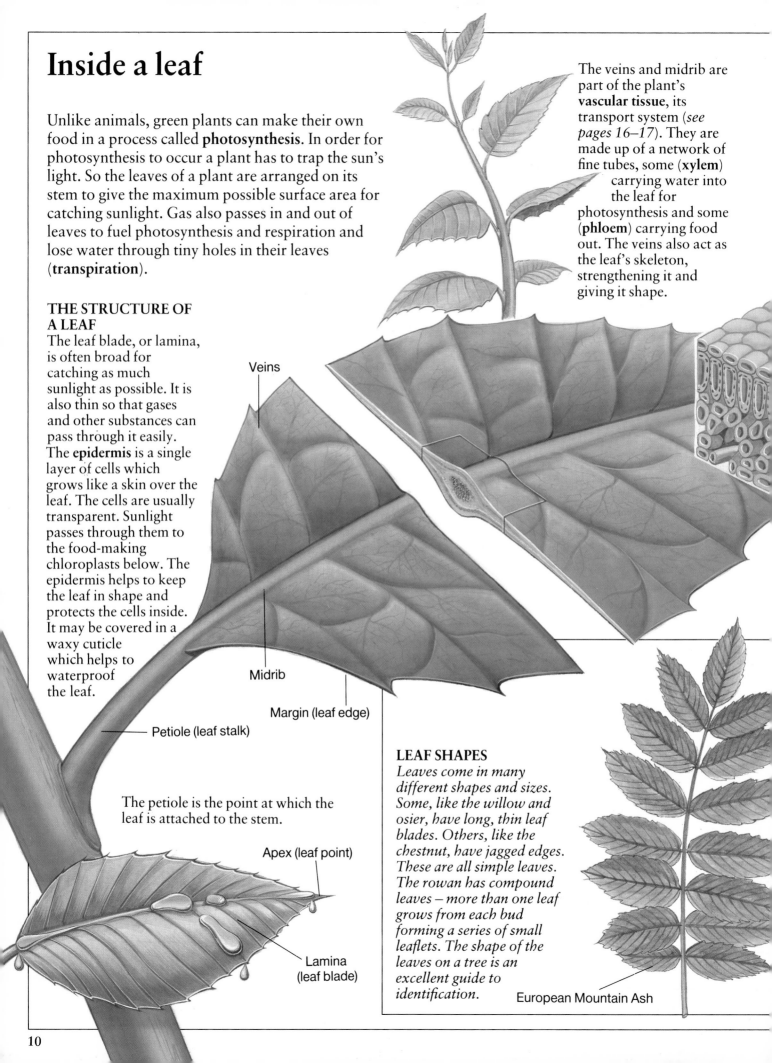

Veins

Midrib

Margin (leaf edge)

Petiole (leaf stalk)

The petiole is the point at which the leaf is attached to the stem.

Apex (leaf point)

Lamina (leaf blade)

## LEAF SHAPES

*Leaves come in many different shapes and sizes. Some, like the willow and osier, have long, thin leaf blades. Others, like the chestnut, have jagged edges. These are all simple leaves. The rowan has compound leaves – more than one leaf grows from each bud forming a series of small leaflets. The shape of the leaves on a tree is an excellent guide to identification.*

European Mountain Ash

10

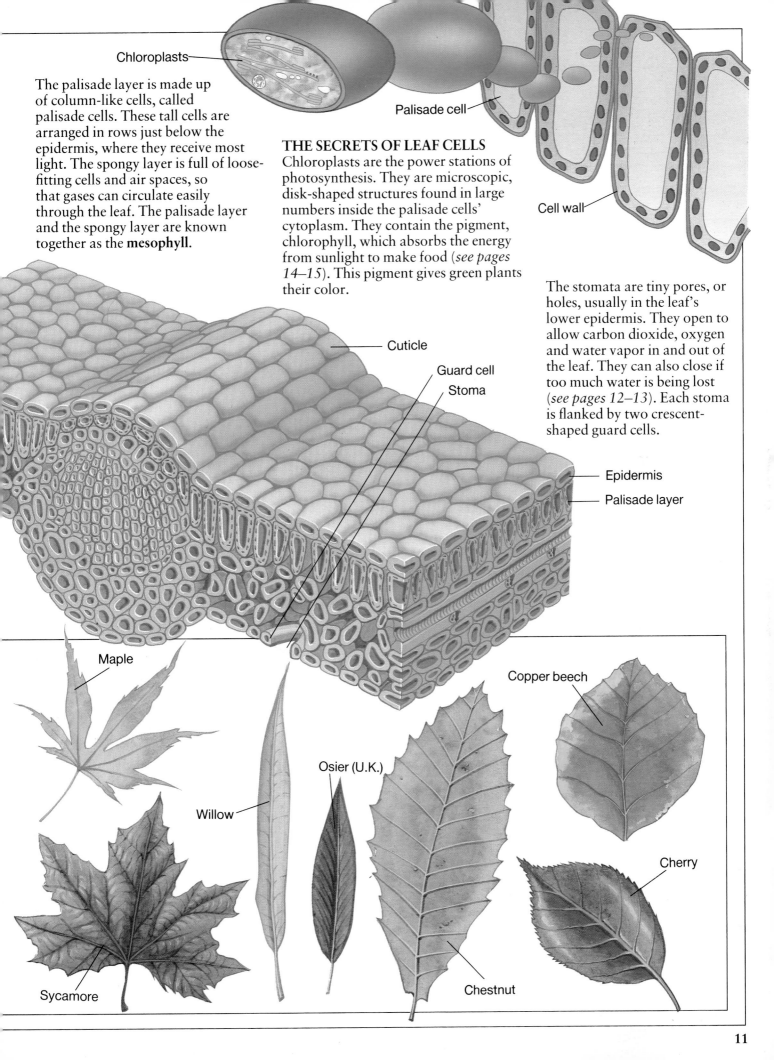

Chloroplasts

The palisade layer is made up of column-like cells, called palisade cells. These tall cells are arranged in rows just below the epidermis, where they receive most light. The spongy layer is full of loose-fitting cells and air spaces, so that gases can circulate easily through the leaf. The palisade layer and the spongy layer are known together as the **mesophyll**.

Palisade cell

Cell wall

## THE SECRETS OF LEAF CELLS
Chloroplasts are the power stations of photosynthesis. They are microscopic, disk-shaped structures found in large numbers inside the palisade cells' cytoplasm. They contain the pigment, chlorophyll, which absorbs the energy from sunlight to make food (*see pages 14–15*). This pigment gives green plants their color.

The stomata are tiny pores, or holes, usually in the leaf's lower epidermis. They open to allow carbon dioxide, oxygen and water vapor in and out of the leaf. They can also close if too much water is being lost (*see pages 12–13*). Each stoma is flanked by two crescent-shaped guard cells.

Cuticle

Guard cell

Stoma

Epidermis

Palisade layer

Maple

Copper beech

Willow

Osier (U.K.)

Cherry

Sycamore

Chestnut

# Stomata – the inside story

The leaf's stomata allow carbon dioxide to enter the leaf for photosynthesis, and oxygen (the waste product) to escape. They also allow oxygen in for respiration, and carbon dioxide (the waste product) out. The stomata are also involved in transpiration.

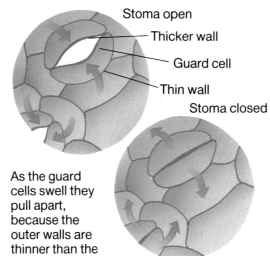

Stoma open
— Thicker wall
— Guard cell
— Thin wall

Stoma closed

As the guard cells swell they pull apart, because the outer walls are thinner than the inner walls.

**OPEN AND CLOSED**
A stoma is opened or closed by its guard cells. A stoma opens when there is a high concentration of sugar in the cell sap of the guard cells. The guard cells take in water from the cells around them, by **osmosis** (*see below*).

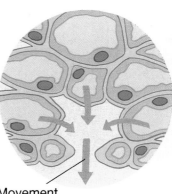

Movement of gases

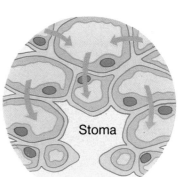

Stoma

*Water is lost from the plant's leaves through the stomata by transpiration.*

## WHAT IS OSMOSIS?

*Osmosis is the way in which water moves from one plant cell to another. If a cell containing a weak solution (a small amount of sugar dissolved in a lot of water) lies next to a cell containing a strong solution (a large amount of sugar in a small amount of water), water molecules will move from the weak to the strong solution by osmosis.*

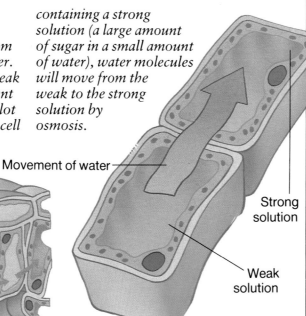

Movement of water

Strong solution

Weak solution

*As water enters the guard cells of the stoma by osmosis it forces the cells apart, and the stoma opens. The stomata are usually open during the day to allow gases in for photosynthesis. However, at night they usually close to prevent too much water being lost.*

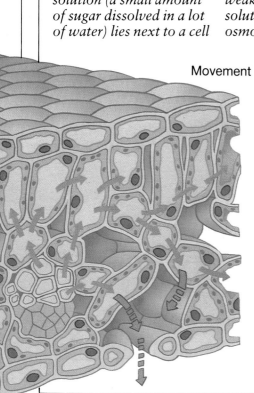

*The water is sucked up the xylem tubes.*

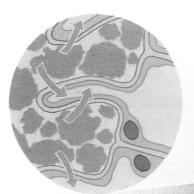

*The roots absorb water from the surrounding soil.*

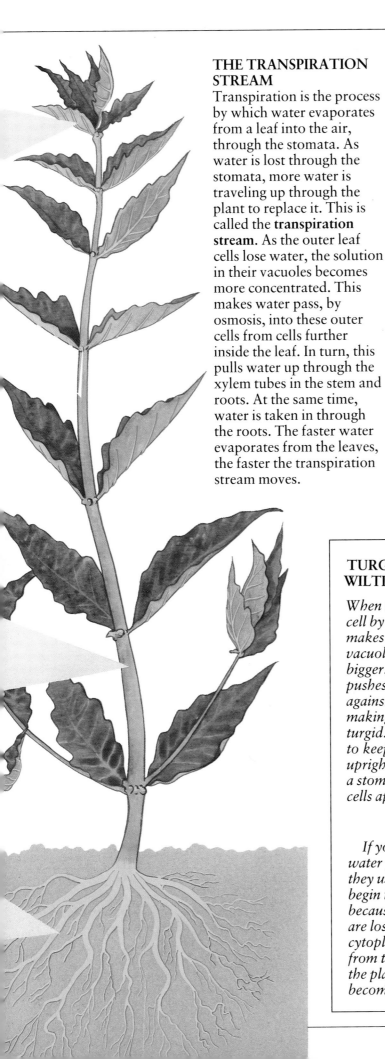

## THE TRANSPIRATION STREAM

Transpiration is the process by which water evaporates from a leaf into the air, through the stomata. As water is lost through the stomata, more water is traveling up through the plant to replace it. This is called the **transpiration stream**. As the outer leaf cells lose water, the solution in their vacuoles becomes more concentrated. This makes water pass, by osmosis, into these outer cells from cells further inside the leaf. In turn, this pulls water up through the xylem tubes in the stem and roots. At the same time, water is taken in through the roots. The faster water evaporates from the leaves, the faster the transpiration stream moves.

## LEAF FACTS

*A large oak tree may have over 25,000 leaves.*

*Cacti spines are a type of leaf. Their needle-like shape stops them from losing precious water in the desert.*

*Many conifer trees also have needle-shaped leaves. The needles of the pine tree have a tough outer layer, and a coating of wax. This allows pines to survive in places that are too dry for many other trees.*

*On a hot, dry day, hundreds of gallons of water may evaporate from a tree's leaves.*

*The raffia palm has the longest leaves of any plant. They can grow up to 65 feet long.*

*During winter it is difficult for trees to draw water from the ground into the roots. Deciduous trees drop their leaves during the winter months so that they do not lose as much water through transpiration. This also helps if there is a heavy fall of snow which would gather on the leaves and could bring down the tree.*

## TURGOR AND WILTING

*When water enters a cell by osmosis, it makes the cell's vacuole swell and get bigger. The vacuole pushes the cytoplasm against the cell wall, making it firm, or turgid.* **Turgor** *helps to keep plant stems upright, and forces a stoma's guard cells apart.*

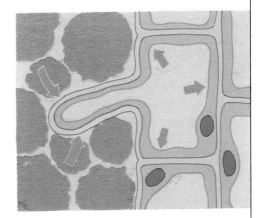

*If you forget to water your pot plants they will, after a time, begin to droop. This is because the vacuoles are losing water. The cytoplasm comes away from the cell wall and the plant wilts and becomes* **flaccid.**

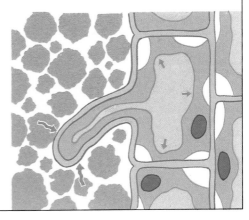

# Making food

Photosynthesis is the chemical process by which green plants make their own food. It happens inside microscopic structures, called chloroplasts, in the cells of the leaves. The chloroplasts contain a green pigment, called chlorophyll. The chlorophyll uses energy from sunlight to combine carbon dioxide from the air with water drawn up through the plant's roots to make molecules of **glucose** (a type of sugar). The sugars are carried around the plant as sap in the phloem tubes (*see page 17*).

**PHOTOSYNTHESIS FACTS**
*Because plants can make their own food, they start off every **food chain**. All animals ultimately rely on plants for food.*

*Algae (simple green plants) produce about two thirds of the oxygen in the air we breathe.*

*In bright light, water molecules inside the chloroplasts are split faster than in dim light.*

*Spirogyra has spiral-shaped chloroplasts. Those in Chlamydomonas are cup-shaped.*

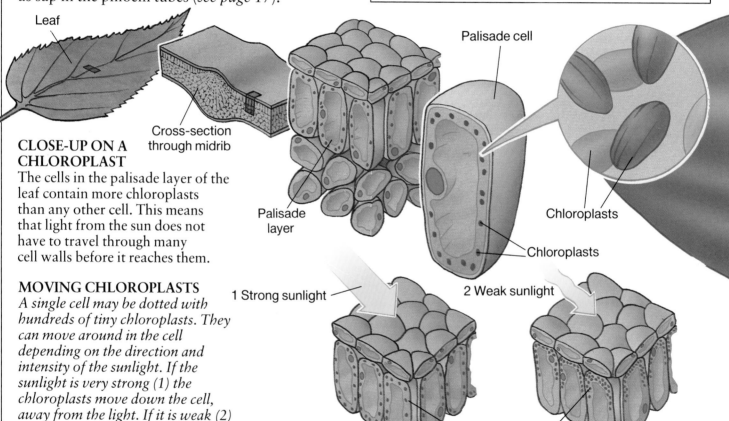

Leaf

Cross-section through midrib

Palisade layer

Palisade cell

Chloroplasts

Chloroplasts

1 Strong sunlight

2 Weak sunlight

Chloroplasts

**CLOSE-UP ON A CHLOROPLAST**
The cells in the palisade layer of the leaf contain more chloroplasts than any other cell. This means that light from the sun does not have to travel through many cell walls before it reaches them.

**MOVING CHLOROPLASTS**
*A single cell may be dotted with hundreds of tiny chloroplasts. They can move around in the cell depending on the direction and intensity of the sunlight. If the sunlight is very strong (1) the chloroplasts move down the cell, away from the light. If it is weak (2) they move up the cell again.*

At night plants respire and take in oxygen and release carbon dioxide.

At dawn the plant begins to photosynthesize.

During the day carbon dioxide is used in photosynthesis, and oxygen is given out.

At dusk photosynthesis stops, but respiration continues through the night.

**RESPIRATION**
*Like animals, plants need oxygen to release energy from their food. This process is called respiration. It uses oxygen and gives out carbon dioxide as a waste product. Respiration continues throughout the night when the plant cannot photosynthesize.*

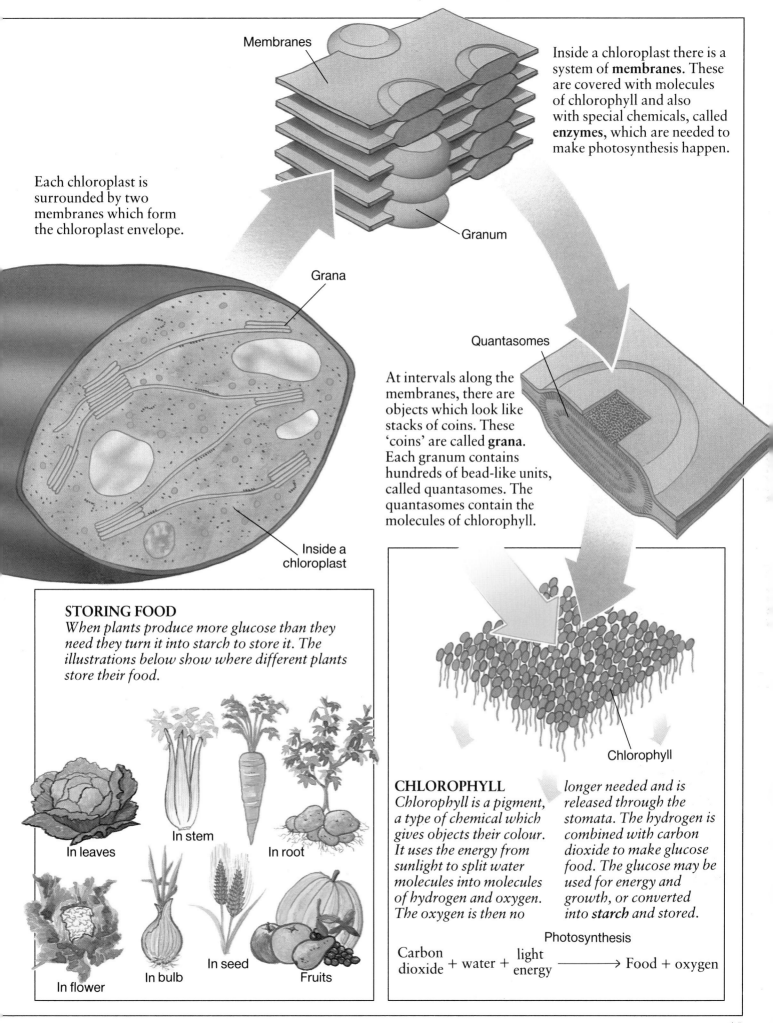

Membranes

Inside a chloroplast there is a system of **membranes**. These are covered with molecules of chlorophyll and also with special chemicals, called **enzymes**, which are needed to make photosynthesis happen.

Each chloroplast is surrounded by two membranes which form the chloroplast envelope.

Granum

Grana

Quantasomes

At intervals along the membranes, there are objects which look like stacks of coins. These 'coins' are called **grana**. Each granum contains hundreds of bead-like units, called quantasomes. The quantasomes contain the molecules of chlorophyll.

Inside a chloroplast

Chlorophyll

**STORING FOOD**
*When plants produce more glucose than they need they turn it into starch to store it. The illustrations below show where different plants store their food.*

In stem

In leaves

In root

In seed

In flower

In bulb

Fruits

**CHLOROPHYLL**
*Chlorophyll is a pigment, a type of chemical which gives objects their colour. It uses the energy from sunlight to split water molecules into molecules of hydrogen and oxygen. The oxygen is then no* *longer needed and is released through the stomata. The hydrogen is combined with carbon dioxide to make glucose food. The glucose may be used for energy and growth, or converted into starch and stored.*

Photosynthesis

Carbon dioxide + water + light energy $\longrightarrow$ Food + oxygen

# Plant plumbing

A plant's stem supports the plant and holds its leaves up to the sunlight. But the stem also contains the plant's plumbing and life-support systems – long bundles of tiny tubes which carry water and food around the plant. One set of tubes, the xylem, carries water and minerals from the roots up the plant to the leaves. The other, the phloem, carries food from the leaves to the rest of the plant. The xylem and phloem form the vascular tissue. Fungi do not have vascular tissue, nor do simple plants such as algae and mosses.

The plumbing system of plants provides much more than just a way of moving fluids around the plant. The xylem is also responsible for supporting the great bulk of plants, particularly in large plants such as trees.

In very large plants there is an added problem. Columns of water are heavy. The weight of a 100 foot high column of water is considerable and the xylem tubes need to be very strong so that they do not burst. It is this that makes wood strong.

**STEM CONSTRUCTION**
The cortex is a tissue layer just inside the epidermis. It is mostly made up of large, loosely packed cells and air spaces. This allows gases to circulate freely. The pith is the inner part of the stem. It is made of the same type of cells as the cortex.

*Sap is a syrupy solution which contains sugars made in the plant's leaves. It flows around the plant transporting food to every part of the plant.*

Between the cortex and the pith lie the **vascular bundles**. Each bundle consists of xylem on the inside and phloem on the outside, with a layer of **cambium** in-between. The cells of the cambium can divide to make new xylem and phloem. The veins in a leaf are off-shoots of the vascular bundles in the stem and the midrib.

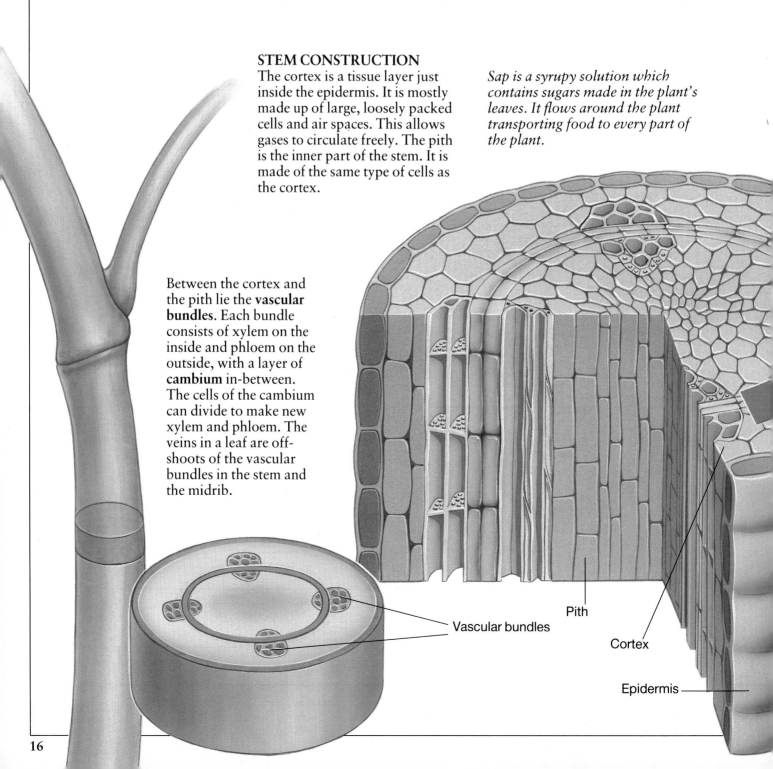

Vascular bundles

Pith

Cortex

Epidermis

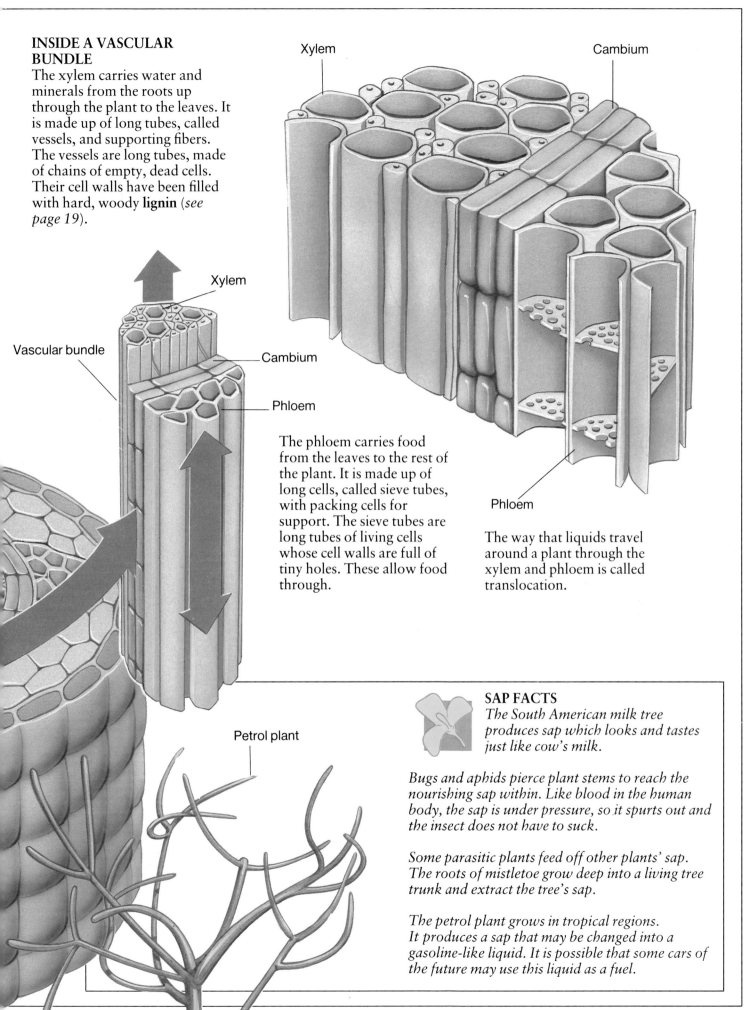

## INSIDE A VASCULAR BUNDLE

The xylem carries water and minerals from the roots up through the plant to the leaves. It is made up of long tubes, called vessels, and supporting fibers. The vessels are long tubes, made of chains of empty, dead cells. Their cell walls have been filled with hard, woody **lignin** (*see page 19*).

Xylem

Cambium

Vascular bundle

Xylem

Cambium

Phloem

Phloem

The phloem carries food from the leaves to the rest of the plant. It is made up of long cells, called sieve tubes, with packing cells for support. The sieve tubes are long tubes of living cells whose cell walls are full of tiny holes. These allow food through.

The way that liquids travel around a plant through the xylem and phloem is called translocation.

Petrol plant

**SAP FACTS**
*The South American milk tree produces sap which looks and tastes just like cow's milk.*

*Bugs and aphids pierce plant stems to reach the nourishing sap within. Like blood in the human body, the sap is under pressure, so it spurts out and the insect does not have to suck.*

*Some parasitic plants feed off other plants' sap. The roots of mistletoe grow deep into a living tree trunk and extract the tree's sap.*

*The petrol plant grows in tropical regions. It produces a sap that may be changed into a gasoline-like liquid. It is possible that some cars of the future may use this liquid as a fuel.*

# What's in wood?

Trees and shrubs are vascular plants but their stems are reinforced with wood. A tree's trunk does exactly the same job as a plant stem. But the extra strength it gets from the wood means that it can grow very tall, towering above other plants in its search for sunlight. A tree's trunk gets thicker each year by producing new vascular tissue for protection, for support, and for carrying fluids up and down the tree.

## GROWING OUTWARDS
*In a young stem (1), the xylem, cambium and phloem are arranged in vascular bundles (see page 17). As the stem gets older and becomes a woody trunk, the cambium grows and joins up (2). The xylem and phloem also join to form a cylinder (3). As more xylem forms, the xylem in the centre of the trunk turns into solid wood (4). It pushes the trunk outwards. The living cells of the phloem are squashed into a thin strip between the bark and the xylem.*

## INSIDE A TREE TRUNK
Instead of an epidermis, a tree trunk is covered in a layer of tough **bark**. It is produced by the cork cambium layer of cells. (*See pages 20–21 for more about bark.*)

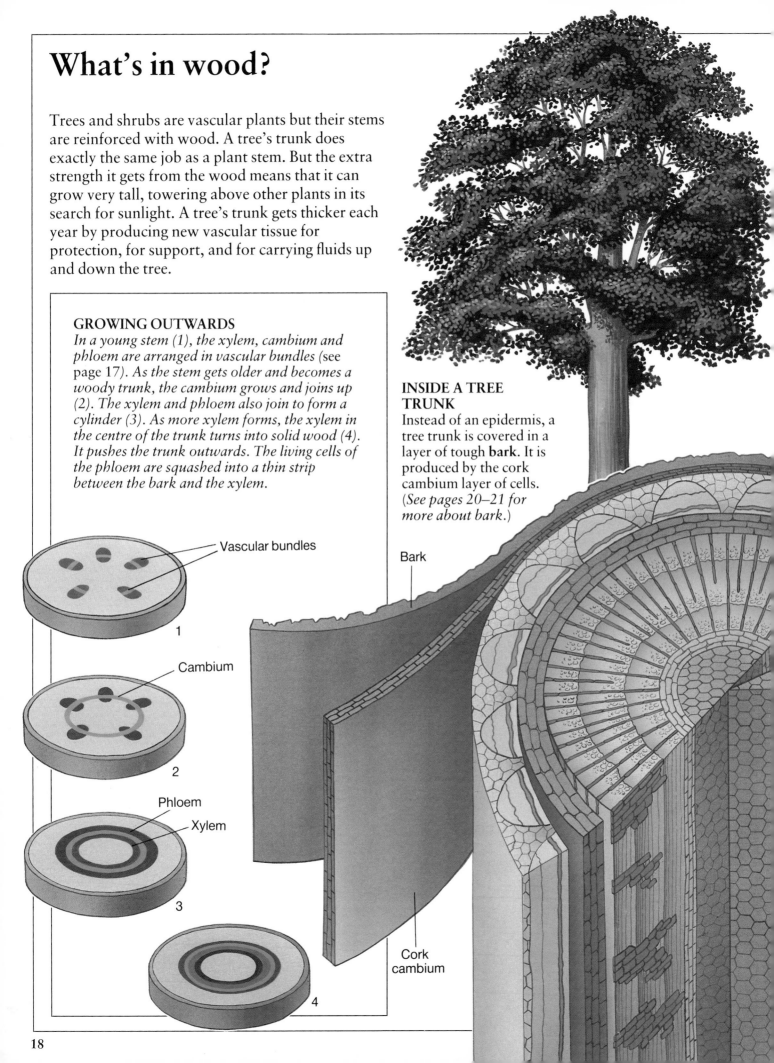

Vascular bundles

1

Cambium

2

Phloem

Xylem

3

4

Bark

Cork cambium

18

Each year, the cells in the cambium divide to produce more xylem on the inside and more phloem on the outside. This makes the trunk thicker.

Lignin is a very strong, hard substance that builds up in the cell walls of the older xylem tubes. It forms a woody barrier which prevents water and nutrients from entering the cells, and so they die. The xylem is now known as wood.

## HEARTWOOD AND SAPWOOD
*As the tree grows the vessels in the oldest, central part of the xylem become filled with woody lignin and die. They can no longer carry water. Their job is to support the trunk. This is the **heartwood**. The younger, outer layer of xylem can still carry water. It is called **sapwood**.*

Phloem
Cambium
Xylem
Medullary ray

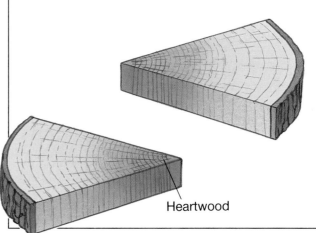

Heartwood

The medullary rays transport water and food across the trunk. They may also store food during the winter.

Xylem

Annual ring

## WOOD FACTS
*The hardness and heaviness of different types of wood depends on how much lignin has built up in the xylem cell walls. The thicker the cell walls, the harder and heavier the wood.*

*The heaviest wood, ironwood, sinks in water. It has very thick cell walls. Balsa wood is light because its cells walls are very thin.*

*On average, trees in temperate climates grow about 1 inch thicker each year.*

*A palm tree's trunk is not made of wood. It consists of tightly-packed leaf bases.*

## TREE RINGS
*The new xylem cells formed by the cambium show up clearly as annual rings in a slice through a tree trunk.*

*Each ring has two sections – the softer, lighter wood that grows in spring, and the harder, darker wood of summer.*

# Bark in focus

A tree's tough, dead layer of bark protects the living layer of sap and water beneath it from animal attack, and from the weather. If a tree's bark is stripped off, the tree will soon die. Some trees have specialized bark. For example, in Australia the eucalyptus tree has bark that protects the inside of the tree from the heat of forest fires.

The bark cambium is a layer of cells towards the outside of the trunk. These cells divide to form a new layer on the inside of the bark cambium and a new layer on the outside.

The new outer layer of cells is called the cork layer. As these cells mature their walls fill up with a fatty substance, called suberin. The suberin stops water and nutrients reaching the cells and they die. These dead cells form the tree's bark.

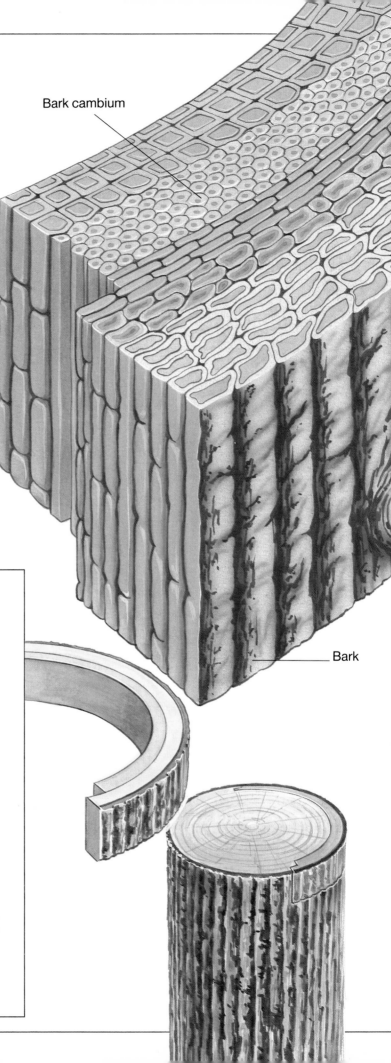

Bark cambium

Bark

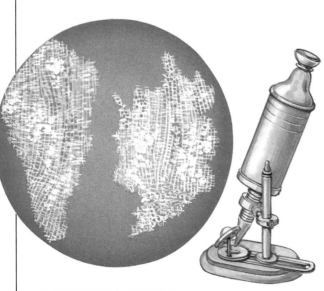

### A SCIENTIFIC FIRST
*This picture of the corky layer of a piece of tree bark was drawn in 1665 by the English scientist, Robert Hooke. It is the first drawing of cells ever made. Robert Hooke was examining the cork under his home-made microscope (above) and noticed that it was made up of hundreds of tiny, box-like blocks.*

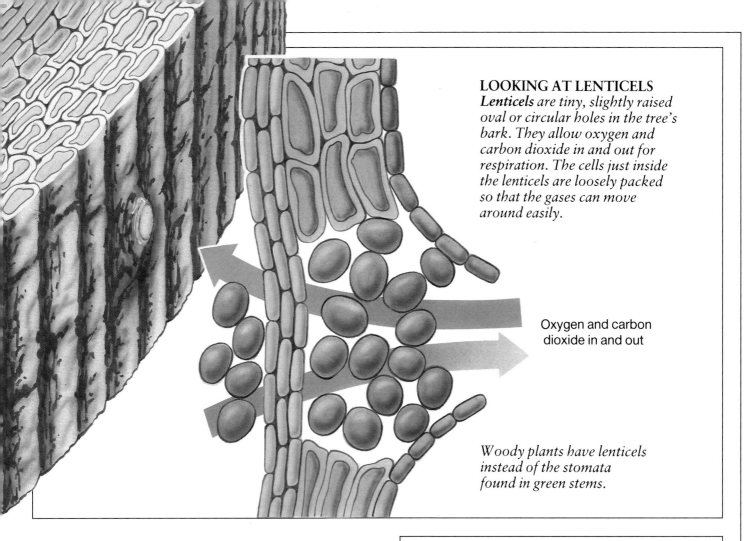

## LOOKING AT LENTICELS

*Lenticels* are tiny, slightly raised oval or circular holes in the tree's bark. They allow oxygen and carbon dioxide in and out for respiration. The cells just inside the lenticels are loosely packed so that the gases can move around easily.

Oxygen and carbon dioxide in and out

*Woody plants have lenticels instead of the stomata found in green stems.*

## BARK FACTS

*Giant sequoia trees have bark over 12 inches thick. The bark on a beech tree, however, is less than 1/4 inch thick.*

*Quinine, a drug used to cure malaria, comes from the bark of the South American cinchona tree.*

*Birch tree bark is papery thin but so tough that it used to be used by North American Indians to make the outer skins of their canoes.*

## BARK PATTERNS

As new cells form in their millions under the dead bark, they push the bark outwards. It cannot stretch so it splits, flakes or cracks. You can identify trees by the characteristic pattern their bark makes. Beech trees, for example, have smooth, flaky bark; oak trees have deep ridges in their bark. Bark on young trees is often smoother than on older trees. Compare the two pictures of the ash tree shown here.

# Rooted to the spot

While a plant's stem and leaves are busy growing up towards the light, its roots grow into the ground, pulled down by the force of **gravity**. The roots have two main functions – to anchor the plant firmly and to absorb water and minerals from the soil for use in photosynthesis. Some plants have very deep roots but most have shallow, spreading roots which can take in water and minerals from a large area of ground.

**GROWING ROOTS**
A plant's roots grow downwards, pulled by the force of gravity. This response to gravity is controlled by a chemical called an **auxin** (*see page 36*). It is made by cells in the tips of the roots.

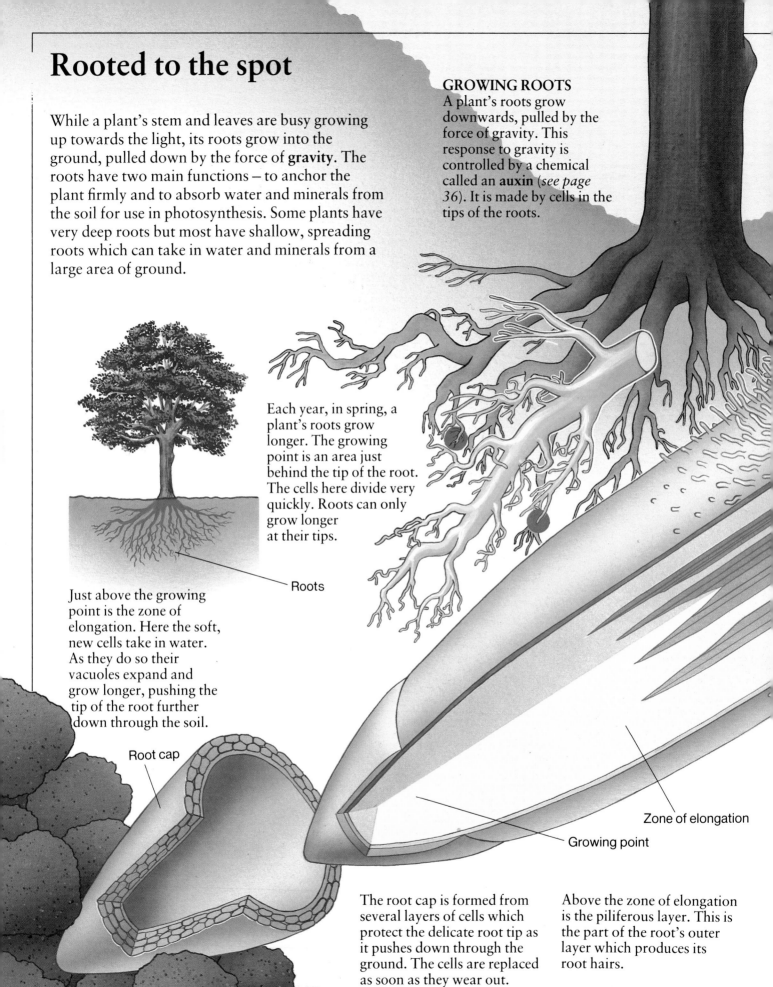

Each year, in spring, a plant's roots grow longer. The growing point is an area just behind the tip of the root. The cells here divide very quickly. Roots can only grow longer at their tips.

Roots

Just above the growing point is the zone of elongation. Here the soft, new cells take in water. As they do so their vacuoles expand and grow longer, pushing the tip of the root further down through the soil.

Root cap

Zone of elongation

Growing point

The root cap is formed from several layers of cells which protect the delicate root tip as it pushes down through the ground. The cells are replaced as soon as they wear out. Cells in the root cap also act as gravity sensors.

Above the zone of elongation is the piliferous layer. This is the part of the root's outer layer which produces its root hairs.

The root's xylem and phloem tubes are grouped in its center. Water and minerals are drawn into the root through the root hairs, then up the xylem to the leaves. The plant food, glucose, is made in the leaves. It passes down the phloem to the growing cells at the tip of the root where it is used to make cellulose for the new cell walls.

Phloem

Xylem

Root hairs

## ROOT FACTS

*The roots of a large oak tree may have to draw over 1,000 gallons of water from the ground each day, in order for the tree to survive.*

*Scientists studying a rye plant calculated that it had grown some 385 miles of roots in just four months.*

*Some rainforest orchids grow on the branches of trees. Their dangling roots absorb moisture from the humid air.*

Rainforest orchid

As the root grows, cells in the piliferous layer produce millions of tiny, tube-like growths, called root hairs. The root hairs stick to the particles of soil, helping the root to grip the soil and anchor the plant more firmly. They also take in minerals, and water by osmosis *(see page 12)*. A plant has so many root hairs that they can double the surface area of the roots, allowing the plant to absorb more water. Root hairs usually only live for about six weeks.

## DIFFERENT TYPES OF ROOT

*There are many different types of root. Plants with tap roots have one main root which grows deep into the soil. Plants with fibrous root systems have a mass of smaller roots growing in all directions.*

*Adventitous roots are additional roots produced from a stem. The mangrove has roots that grow above water to absorb oxygen from the air.*

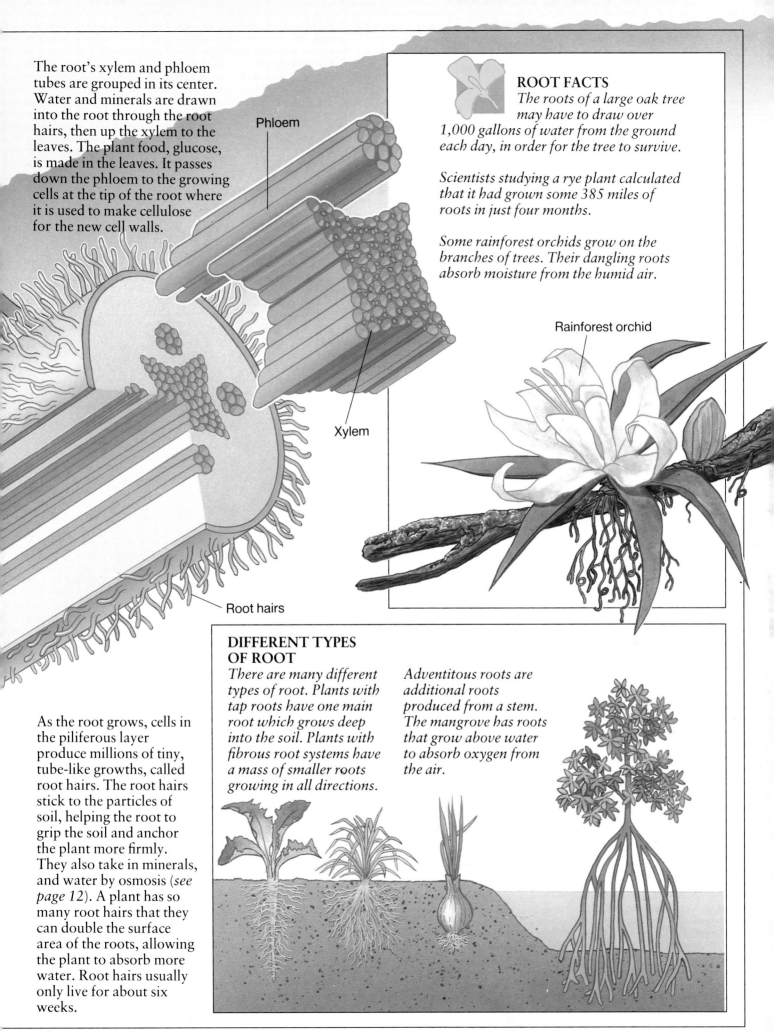

# Journey through a flower

Many plants produce an amazing array of flowers, from tiny florets to bizarre bee-shaped orchids. Many flowers are brightly colored or have strong, sweet scents. These features are not simply for show. They are all designed to entice insects and other creatures to the flowers for **pollination** (*see page 30*). Flowers contain a plant's male and female reproductive parts with the male and female sex cells inside. These sex cells must be brought together to develop into seeds.

**FLOWER STRUCTURE**
The flower grows at the enlarged end of the flower stalk, called the receptacle. The sepals grow in a ring around the petals to protect the flower bud as it develops. They are usually small and green. But if they look identical to the petals, they are known as tepals.

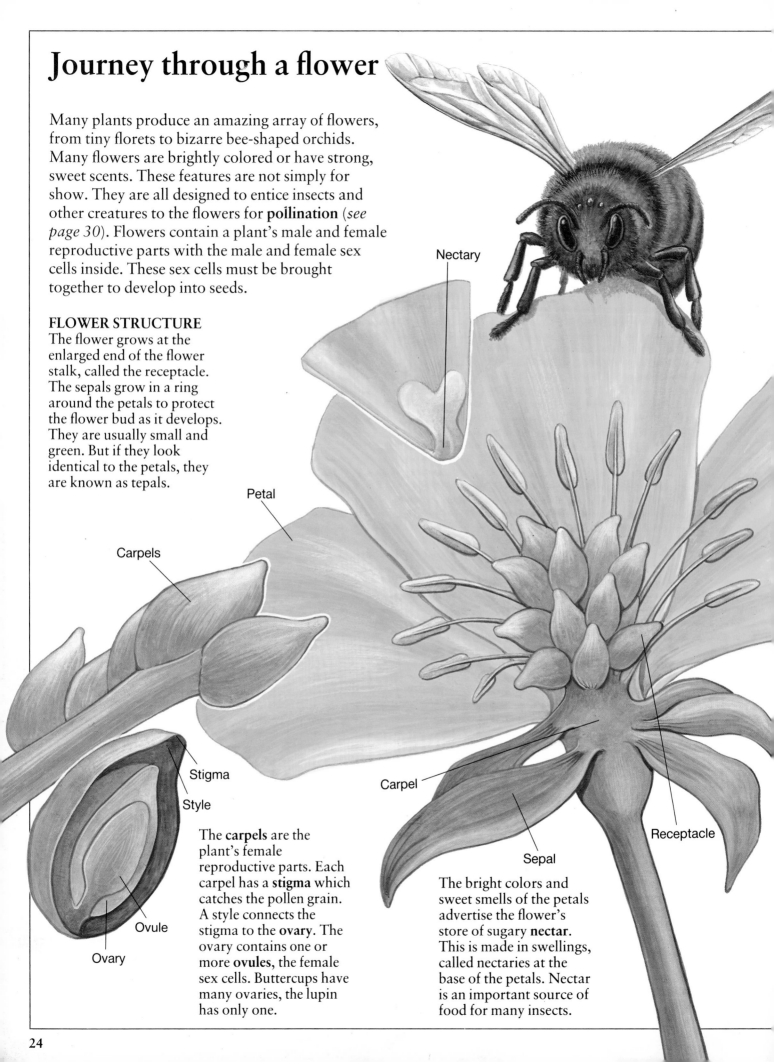

Nectary

Petal

Carpels

Stigma

Style

Ovule

Ovary

Carpel

Sepal

Receptacle

The **carpels** are the plant's female reproductive parts. Each carpel has a **stigma** which catches the pollen grain. A style connects the stigma to the **ovary**. The ovary contains one or more **ovules**, the female sex cells. Buttercups have many ovaries, the lupin has only one.

The bright colors and sweet smells of the petals advertise the flower's store of sugary **nectar**. This is made in swellings, called nectaries at the base of the petals. Nectar is an important source of food for many insects.

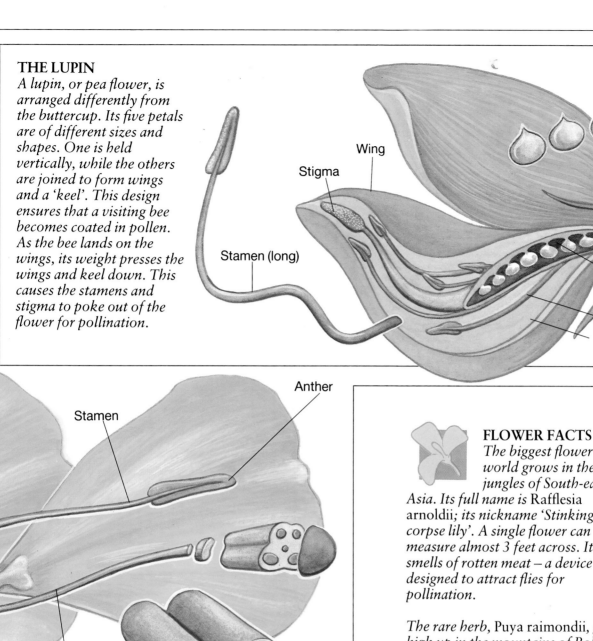

## THE LUPIN

*A lupin, or pea flower, is arranged differently from the buttercup. Its five petals are of different sizes and shapes. One is held vertically, while the others are joined to form wings and a 'keel'. This design ensures that a visiting bee becomes coated in pollen. As the bee lands on the wings, its weight presses the wings and keel down. This causes the stamens and stigma to poke out of the flower for pollination.*

Ovule

Wing

Stigma

Stamen (long)

Ovary

Stamen (short)

Keel

Anther

Stamen

Filament

Pollen sac

The **stamens** are the male parts of the plant. Each consists of a stalk-like filament, topped by an **anther**. The anther contains four **pollen** sacs which burst and release tiny grains of pollen, the male sex cells (*see pages 30–31*).

Filament

Pollen released

Pollen

## FLOWER FACTS

*The biggest flower in the world grows in the jungles of South-east Asia. Its full name is* Rafflesia arnoldii; *its nickname 'Stinking corpse lily'. A single flower can measure almost 3 feet across. It smells of rotten meat – a device designed to attract flies for pollination.*

*The rare herb,* Puya raimondii, *grows high up in the mountains of Bolivia. It does not produce its first flowers until it is 80 to 150 years old. Then it grows the tallest flower head known – a spike over 33 feet high.*

*The first flowers grew about 100 million years ago. From fossils, it seems that they were similar to modern magnolia flowers.*

Raffelesia

# Beautiful colors

Plants get their colors from special chemicals, called pigments, inside their cells. Apart from chlorophyll (*see page 15*), plants contain hundreds of other pigments which are displayed to their best effect in the beautiful colors of flowers and autumn leaves. These colors have an important role to play. Many flowers that are pollinated by insects, bats or birds rely on bright colors to attract their pollinators to them. The change of colors in an autumn leaf is part of the tree's preparations for surviving the winter.

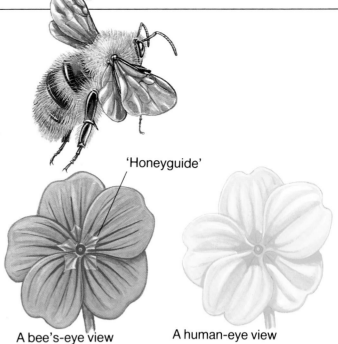

'Honeyguide'

A bee's-eye view    A human-eye view

### INSIDE A CHROMOPLAST
Some of a plant's pigments are contained in plastids, called **chromoplasts**, in its cells. Other pigments are dissolved in the cell sap.

### A BEE'S-EYE VIEW
A bee visiting this primrose to collect pollen does not see it as we do. Bees can detect **ultraviolet (UV) light** which we cannot see. So, the yellow primrose looks blue to the bee. In UV light, the 'honeyguide' markings on the petals are also clearer. They are thought to guide the bee towards the nectar.

### YELLOW TO RED
Different pigments absorb and reflect different parts of the visible spectrum, which is why plants appear to be different colors. **Carotenoids**, for example, reflect yellow, orange and red light so they make flowers and fruit look yellow, orange or red. Carotenoids are found in a cell's chromoplasts. They range from pale daffodil yellow to rich tomato red.

The bee orchid not only looks and smells like a female bee it feels like one too. Its disguise has evolved over millions of years to attract male bees for pollination.

Bee orchid

### PINK TO PURPLE
*Anthocyanins are pigments that range from pale pink to deep purple. They are dissolved in the plant's cell sap and are affected by how acidic the sap is. This is why hydrangeas produce pink flowers in alkaline soil, but blue flowers in acidic soil.*

Acidic soil    Alkaline soil

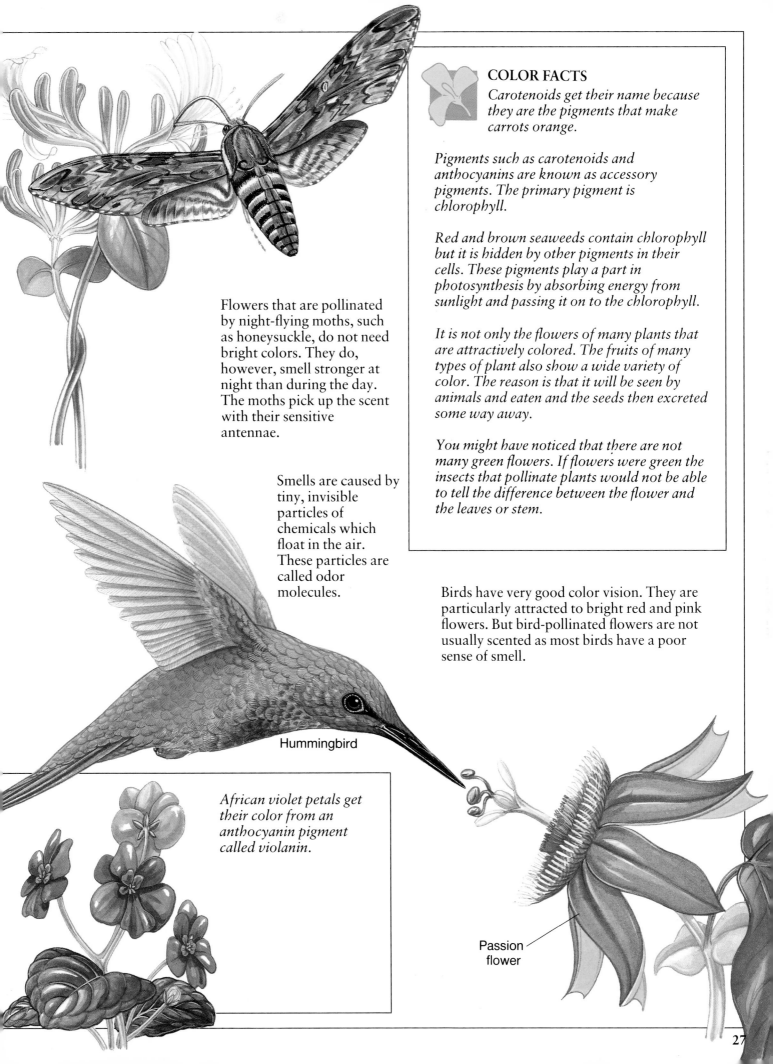

Flowers that are pollinated by night-flying moths, such as honeysuckle, do not need bright colors. They do, however, smell stronger at night than during the day. The moths pick up the scent with their sensitive antennae.

Smells are caused by tiny, invisible particles of chemicals which float in the air. These particles are called odor molecules.

## COLOR FACTS

*Carotenoids get their name because they are the pigments that make carrots orange.*

*Pigments such as carotenoids and anthocyanins are known as accessory pigments. The primary pigment is chlorophyll.*

*Red and brown seaweeds contain chlorophyll but it is hidden by other pigments in their cells. These pigments play a part in photosynthesis by absorbing energy from sunlight and passing it on to the chlorophyll.*

*It is not only the flowers of many plants that are attractively colored. The fruits of many types of plant also show a wide variety of color. The reason is that it will be seen by animals and eaten and the seeds then excreted some way away.*

*You might have noticed that there are not many green flowers. If flowers were green the insects that pollinate plants would not be able to tell the difference between the flower and the leaves or stem.*

Birds have very good color vision. They are particularly attracted to bright red and pink flowers. But bird-pollinated flowers are not usually scented as most birds have a poor sense of smell.

Hummingbird

*African violet petals get their color from an anthocyanin pigment called violanin.*

Passion flower

# Autumn colors

The dramatic change from bushy green foliage, through the yellows, reds and russets of autumn to the bare branches of winter enables **deciduous** trees to survive the winter months. If the leaves remained on the tree through the winter, they would lose more water by transpiration (*see page 13*) than the roots could absorb from the cold ground. So the leaves would die anyway and precious energy would have been wasted.

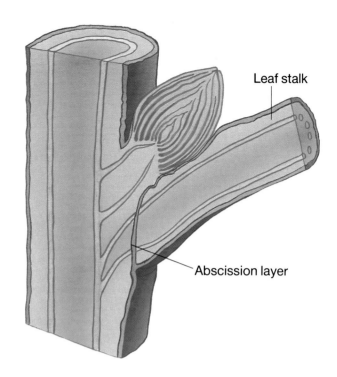

Leaf stalk

Abscission layer

## HIDDEN COLORS

The changes in color of the leaves on a deciduous tree are caused by changes in the balance of pigments inside the leaves. In the summer, the green chlorophyll hides the other pigments in the leaves. These include the carotenoids (oranges, yellows and reds) and the anthocyanins (purples and blues). The tree can sense that autumn is approaching as the days get shorter and there is less light for photosynthesis. It prepares to shed its leaves. The cells at the base of each leaf stalk divide and form a corky wall of tissue. This is called the abscission layer. No water can reach the leaf and it begins to die.

As the leaf dies, any sugars trapped inside begin to break down and a chain of chemical reactions causes the balance of pigments to change. The green chlorophyll is destroyed and the reds, yellows, oranges and mauves of the other pigments show through in a glorious blaze of color.

Summer foliage

Autumn colors

## FALLING OFF

The leaf eventually falls off, leaving a scar on the twig. The leaf scar has a pattern of tiny dots made by the vascular bundles. This pattern varies for every different **species** of tree.

Breakage point

Leaf stalk

Bark

Stem

Leaf scar

## EVERGREENS

*Evergreen* trees do not need to shed their leaves to survive the winter. Conifer needles have a small surface area so they do not lose as much water as broad leaves. Holly leaves have a waxy cuticle to prevent them from drying out.

## BUDS

The tree survives the winter in a state very much like hibernation. When the warmer, spring weather arrives, the tree's buds burst and its new leaves grow and begin to make food.

## GIRDLE SCARS

The bud growing at the end of the twig is called the leader bud. It grows faster than the other side buds, increasing the length of the twig. Each year's leader bud leaves a scar, called a girdle scar, on the twig. The distance between two girdle scars shows how much a twig has grown in one year.

Girdle scars

Bare winter branches

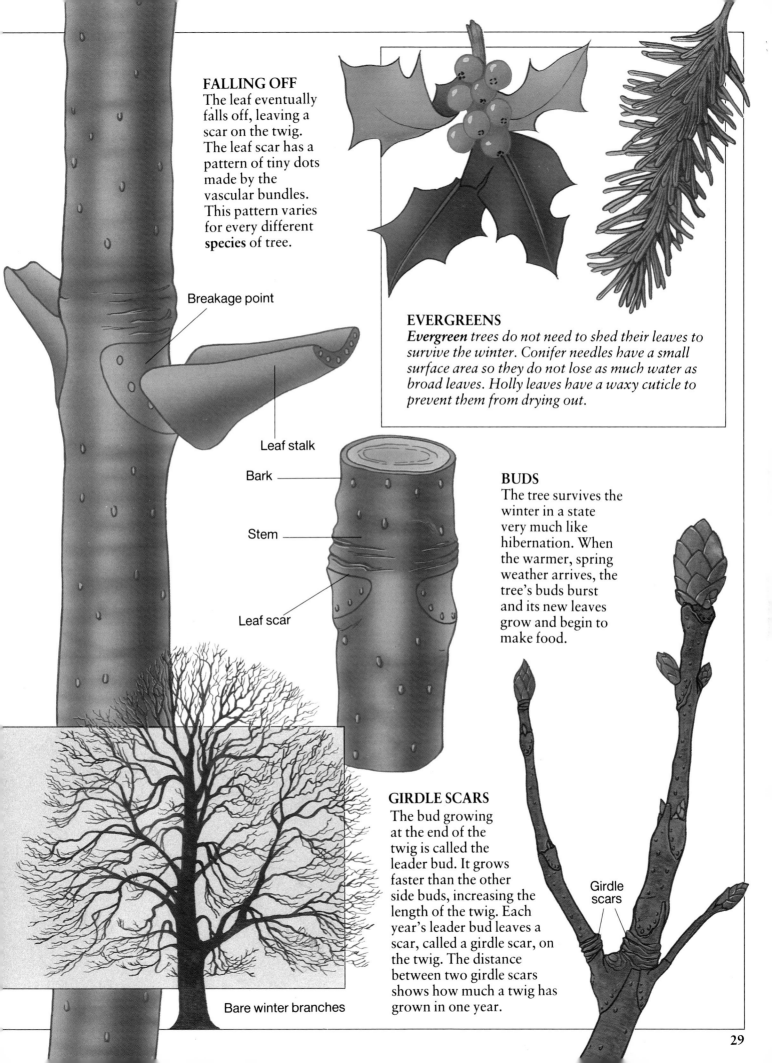

# Pollen precision

Each of a plant's pollen grains contains a male sex cell. Each of its ovules contains a female sex cell. For a seed to develop and form a new plant, the male and female sex cells must join together. This is called **fertilization**. First, however, the pollen has to be transferred to the female parts of a flower. This process is called pollination. Pollination may be carried out by insects, birds, water or the wind.

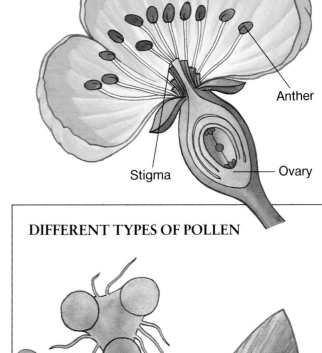

Anther

Stigma

Ovary

## POLLINATION IN PROGRESS

1. The pollen grains are made and stored inside four sacs in the anther. When the anther is ripe, its walls dry up and shrink. The tension builds up until the anther suddenly splits apart, releasing thousands or even millions of tiny grains.

2. Each pollen grain has two nuclei. One is called the tube nucleus. It controls the growth of the pollen tube. The second nucleus is called the generative nucleus. It splits in two to form two male nuclei when the pollen grain reaches the stigma.

## DIFFERENT TYPES OF POLLEN

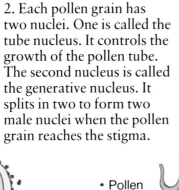

Pollen sac

Pollen

*Flowers which use insects for pollination usually produce spiky pollen grains so that the grains will stick to the insects' bodies. Wind-pollinated flowers produce smaller, smoother grains, but in huge numbers so that at least a few survive.*

Anther

Stamen

Pollen

Stigma

## BEE POLLINATION

A bee visits a flower to feed, and its body gets dusted with pollen. It then flies to another flower. Here the pollen from the bee's body sticks to the female stigma, the top of the carpel.

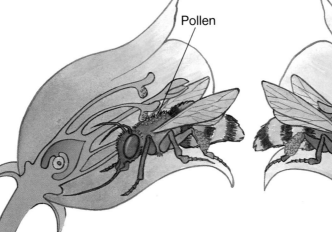

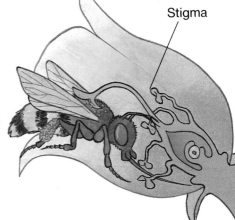

3. Once the pollen grain has been transported to the female stigma it absorbs a nourishing sugary liquid from the stigma. It then grows a long tube which reaches down the style and into the ovary. The tube enters the ovule through a small hole, called a **micropyle**.

Pollen

Stigma

4. The pollen grain's two male nuclei (formed from the generative nucleus) travel down the tube and into the ovule. There one of the nuclei joins, or fuses, with the nucleus of the female egg cell to form a new cell which then divides to make an embryo. The other nucleus fuses with two other cells in the ovule to form a food store around the embryo.

Egg cell

Male cell

Style

Pollen tube

Ovary

Ovule

Egg cell nucleus

Pollen nucleus

Seed

Fruit

5. The fertilized ovule now becomes a seed and the ovary develops into a **fruit** around it. The flower's job is done and its petals turn brown, shrivel up and die.

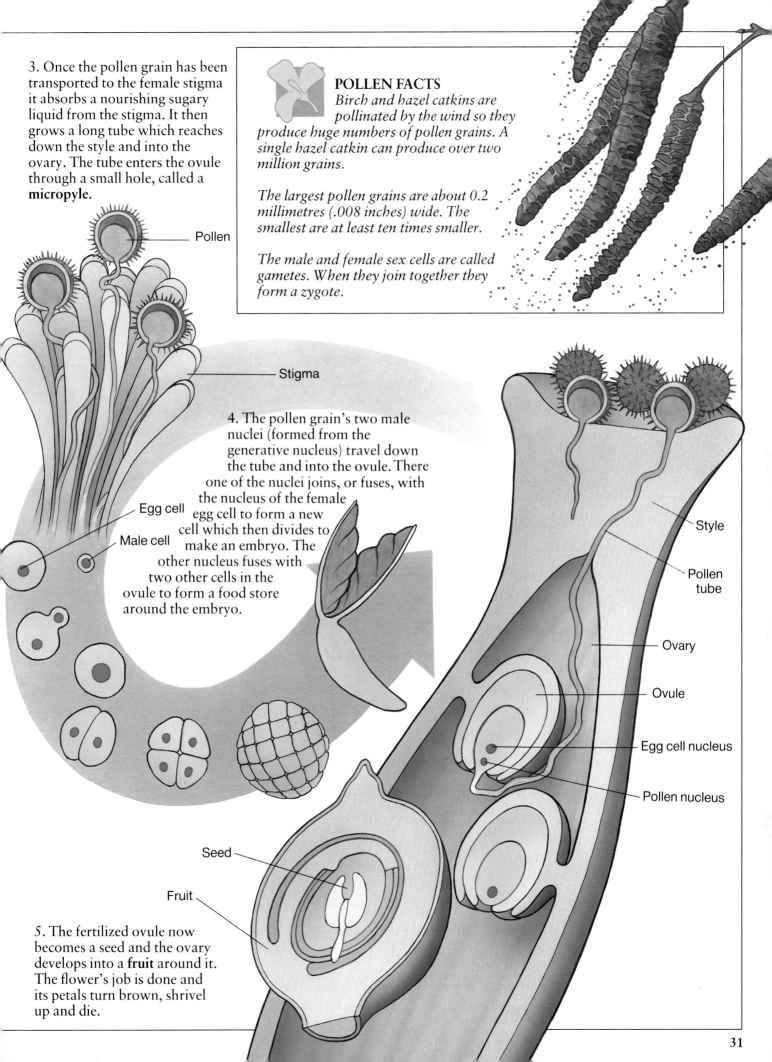

31

# The secret of seeds

When the pollen in a flowering plant has fertilized the ovule, the ovule becomes a seed. It contains the beginnings of a new plant and a store of food. The plant cannot make food for itself until its leaves have grown. The ovary develops into a protective fruit around the seed. Pods, nuts and berries are all fruits. The seeds need to travel away from their parent plant to avoid competition for space and light. As with pollination, plants rely on animals, wind and water for seed dispersal.

**SEEDS ON THE MOVE**
A fruit's size and shape are clues as to how its seeds are dispersed. Wind-borne seeds are very light. Their fruits may have wings to catch currents of air. They include dandelion parachutes and sycamore keys.

Some fruits act as natural catapults and shoot out their seeds. Broom, laburnum and lupin seeds grow in pods. As the fibers in the pod wall dry in the sun they shrink and become tense, like a piece of elastic pulled tight. Suddenly the fibers snap and the pod splits apart, sending its seeds shooting out.

Some plants produce fleshy fruits, such as blackberries or cherries. Birds find their juiciness and sweetness irresistible. The seeds or pips pass unharmed through the birds' bodies and out again.

Burdock and goosegrass fruits are covered in tiny hooks, which catch on the wool, fur or skin of passing animals.

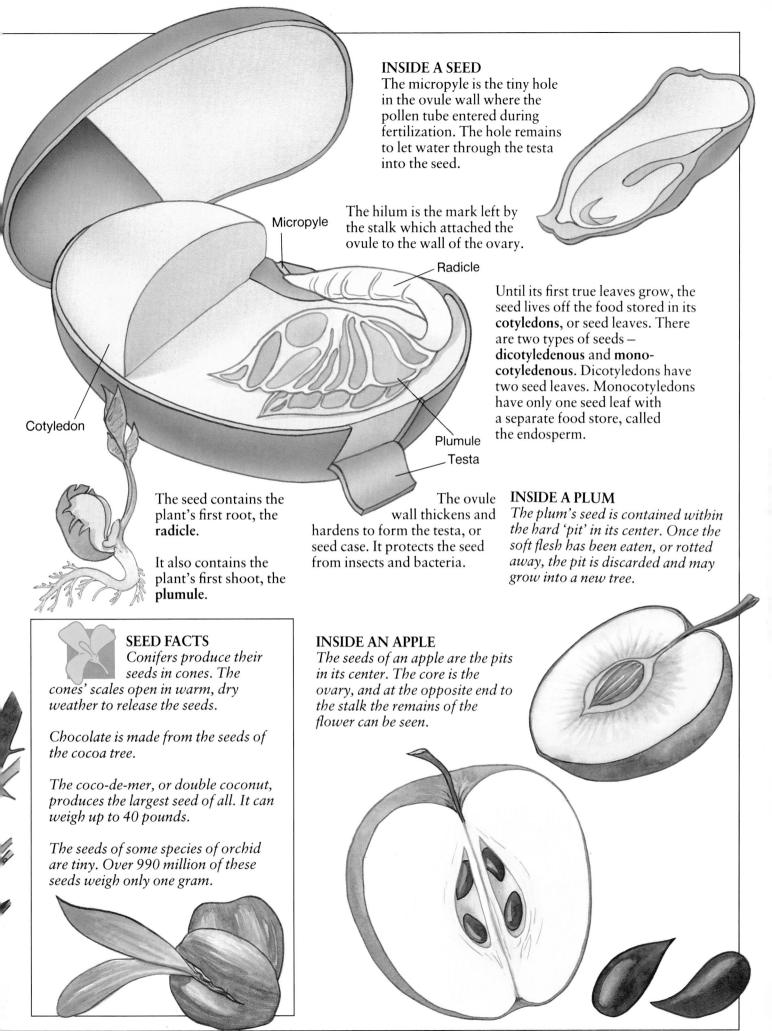

## INSIDE A SEED

The micropyle is the tiny hole in the ovule wall where the pollen tube entered during fertilization. The hole remains to let water through the testa into the seed.

Micropyle

The hilum is the mark left by the stalk which attached the ovule to the wall of the ovary.

Radicle

Until its first true leaves grow, the seed lives off the food stored in its **cotyledons**, or seed leaves. There are two types of seeds – **dicotyledenous** and **mono-cotyledenous**. Dicotyledons have two seed leaves. Monocotyledons have only one seed leaf with a separate food store, called the endosperm.

Cotyledon

Plumule

Testa

The seed contains the plant's first root, the **radicle**.

It also contains the plant's first shoot, the **plumule**.

The ovule wall thickens and hardens to form the testa, or seed case. It protects the seed from insects and bacteria.

## INSIDE A PLUM

*The plum's seed is contained within the hard 'pit' in its center. Once the soft flesh has been eaten, or rotted away, the pit is discarded and may grow into a new tree.*

## SEED FACTS

*Conifers produce their seeds in cones. The cones' scales open in warm, dry weather to release the seeds.*

*Chocolate is made from the seeds of the cocoa tree.*

*The coco-de-mer, or double coconut, produces the largest seed of all. It can weigh up to 40 pounds.*

*The seeds of some species of orchid are tiny. Over 990 million of these seeds weigh only one gram.*

## INSIDE AN APPLE

*The seeds of an apple are the pits in its center. The core is the ovary, and at the opposite end to the stalk the remains of the flower can be seen.*

# Growing up

The process by which a seed grows into a new plant is called germination. After leaving its parent plant, a seed may lie dormant (or inactive) for weeks or even months until conditions are right for it to grow. This often means lying dormant over winter and being triggered into life by the warmth, sunlight and moisture brought by the beginning of spring.

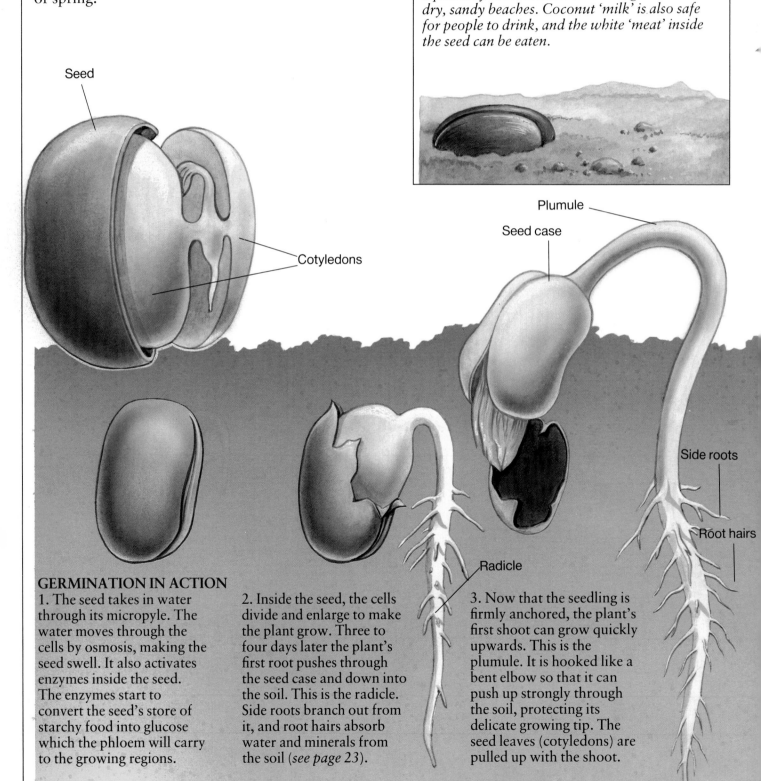

Seed

Cotyledons

Plumule

Seed case

Side roots

Root hairs

Radicle

**GERMINATION IN ACTION**
1. The seed takes in water through its micropyle. The water moves through the cells by osmosis, making the seed swell. It also activates enzymes inside the seed. The enzymes start to convert the seed's store of starchy food into glucose which the phloem will carry to the growing regions.

2. Inside the seed, the cells divide and enlarge to make the plant grow. Three to four days later the plant's first root pushes through the seed case and down into the soil. This is the radicle. Side roots branch out from it, and root hairs absorb water and minerals from the soil (*see page 23*).

3. Now that the seedling is firmly anchored, the plant's first shoot can grow quickly upwards. This is the plumule. It is hooked like a bent elbow so that it can push up strongly through the soil, protecting its delicate growing tip. The seed leaves (cotyledons) are pulled up with the shoot.

First true leaves

4. Once above ground, the plumule straightens and the plant's first leaves begin to grow. The seed leaves shrivel and fall off as their food store is used up.

5. The leaves get bigger and turn greener as chlorophyll develops inside them. They can now make their own food by photosynthesis (*see page 14*). The cells at the tip of the stem continue to divide and make the stem longer.

**INSIDE A FLOWER BUD**
*All the various parts of the flower are packed tightly inside the bud and protected by the sepals. When conditions are right, the bud bursts open. The petals grow and open out to expose the anthers and stigma.*

Overlapping leaves

**INSIDE A LEAF BUD**
The bud containing a tree's new leaf is usually protected by tough leaves, called bud scales. Like seeds, most buds lie dormant over winter and open in the warmer spring weather. The bud scales protect them from drying out and from attack by birds and insects. In spring, the cells at the tip of the stem divide and grow longer. They force the bud scales open. The leaves open out and can start photosynthesizing almost immediately.

**BURSTING INTO BUD**
Packed tightly inside a tiny bud are all the parts needed to produce a new flower or leaf. A bud is actually a type of shoot, with a short stem and leaves or petals wrapped around each other.

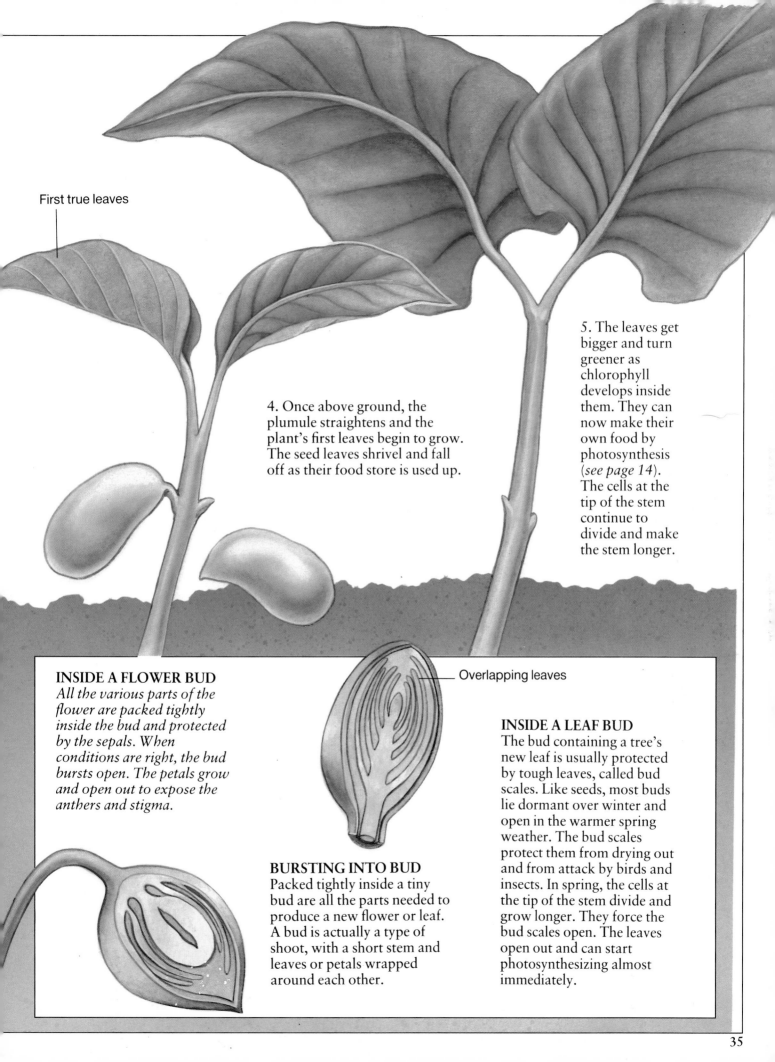

# Sensitive plants

Plants cannot see, hear or feel things in the way that humans do, nor can they get up and move from place to place. But they do react to some types of stimulation such as the direction of sunlight, and the pull of gravity. Their responses often involve movement brought about by growing slowly, for example towards or away from light. These responses are called **tropisms**. They are controlled and co-ordinated by special chemicals. The best known are called auxins.

## PHOTOTROPISM

Phototropism is a plant's reaction to light. Wherever they are, plants will point their stems and leaves in order to face the light.

Auxins are special chemicals produced in the growing tips of the stems and roots. Auxins control how the plant grows. They do this by delaying the formation of a rigid cell wall, allowing water to be drawn into the cells by osmosis. The vacuole becomes enlarged so that it presses out against the cell wall and the cell grows longer.

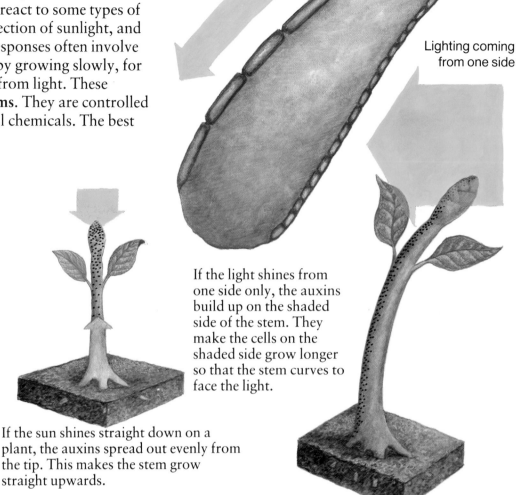

Auxin

Lighting coming from one side

If the light shines from one side only, the auxins build up on the shaded side of the stem. They make the cells on the shaded side grow longer so that the stem curves to face the light.

If the sun shines straight down on a plant, the auxins spread out evenly from the tip. This makes the stem grow straight upwards.

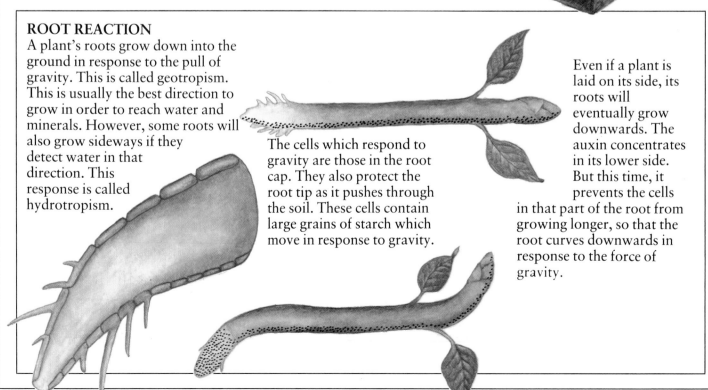

## ROOT REACTION

A plant's roots grow down into the ground in response to the pull of gravity. This is called geotropism. This is usually the best direction to grow in order to reach water and minerals. However, some roots will also grow sideways if they detect water in that direction. This response is called hydrotropism.

The cells which respond to gravity are those in the root cap. They also protect the root tip as it pushes through the soil. These cells contain large grains of starch which move in response to gravity.

Even if a plant is laid on its side, its roots will eventually grow downwards. The auxin concentrates in its lower side. But this time, it prevents the cells in that part of the root from growing longer, so that the root curves downwards in response to the force of gravity.

## OPENING AND CLOSING TIMES

Plants have an in-built clock which can tell the time of year and day. It reacts mainly to the length of the nights and controls the development and opening times of the plant's flowers. This response is called photo-periodism. It ensures that flowers open at times when they stand the best chance of being pollinated.

Some plants are called short-day plants, for example, chrysanthemums. They only flower when the days are shorter than a certain length, called the critical length.

Long-day plants, such as carnations, only flower when the days are longer than the critical length.

Day-neutral plants, such as snap-dragons, are not affected by the length of the day.

Botanists think that the instructions for a plant to flower at a particular time are given by a chemical, called phytochrome, produced in the leaves. The petals open when the cells in the petals take in water and become turgid (*see page 13*).

(*see page 13*)

### SENSITIVE FACTS

*Some wheat seeds which were germinated on board a space station grew into healthy plants except that their shoots and roots grew completely haphazardly. Because the seeds were germinated in zero gravity and in darkness, they became disorientated.*

*The word 'auxin' comes from the Greek word, auxein, which means 'to increase'.*

*The function of auxins was first discovered by the English scientist, Charles Darwin, in a series of experiments on oat seedlings.*

*Plants are sensitive to other stimuli apart from gravity and light. The roots are sensitive to water and will grow towards the nearest water source. This is particularly important in dry areas where water may be scarce and where growing straight down may not always find a good source of water.*

*Some plants, such as daisies, have flowers which open during the day and close at night, as if they are sleeping. This may also be linked with changes in turgor and in the rate at which the plant is growing.*

Tulip flowers close at night because the lower edges of their petals grow more quickly than the upper edges. This pattern is reversed to allow the flowers to open in the morning.

Daisies

Tulips

# Touch sensitive

Some plants are sensitive to touch. This is known as haptotropism. Some respond by growing, others by moving – often very quickly indeed. **Carnivorous** plants, such as the Venus fly-trap, use this rapid reaction to trap their food. Other plants, such as the mimosa, seem to use movement as a form of defense. Like the other forms of tropism (*see pages 36–7*), haptotropism is controlled by auxins.

**TOUCH FACTS**
*A Venus fly-trap trap dies after it has caught and digested three fly-sized insects.*

*A Mimosa pudica collapses at a rate of one inch per second.*

*The leaves of the sundew plant are covered in sticky hairs. Insects get glued to the leaves which fold over to digest them. The biggest sundews have leaves up to two feet long.*

### TENDRIL TOUCH
Sweet peas are climbing plants. They climb up towards the light with the help of sticks or other plant stems for support. Long tendrils grow from their stems. When a tendril touches a support its touch-sensitive tip starts to twist and curl around.

Gradually, the rest of the tendril coils up behind the tip like a spring, bringing the plant closer to its support. The 'spring' allows the tendril to stretch in the wind, instead of being snapped.

Sweet pea

Stick support

Tendril

Touch-sensitive tip

'Spring'

### IN A STATE OF COLLAPSE
The Mimosa pudica *is also known as the 'sensitive plant'. If it is touched, it responds by wilting rapidly. This is thought to be a defense mechanism for shaking off any insects feeding on the plant's leaves.*

*The mimosa has compound leaves, with lots of small leaflets arranged on a stalk. At the base of each leaflet, there is a swelling containing lots of large, thin-walled cells. Any slight touch causes water to drain out of these cells and they wilt, making the leaflet drop down.*

*The plant can collapse in just a few seconds. But it takes several hours for it to return to its normal turgid state.*

## SPRINGING A TRAP

Carnivorous plants, such as the Venus fly-trap, can photosynthesize and make their own food. However, they also supplement their diets with insects and other small animals. The Venus fly-trap's leaves are formed from two pads, joined by a fluid-filled hinge and fringed with stiff spikes. The pads lie open, waiting for an insect to land.

When an insect lands, it brushes against three touch-sensitive bristles on each leaf surface (1). This sets off a chain reaction. The fluid pours out of the hinge, the cells wilt and the trap shuts. It takes less than a second for the trap to shut enough for the insect to be unable to escape (2).

Once the trap is fully closed, acids and enzymes from cells inside the leaves begin to dissolve the insect (3). The soft parts are absorbed by the leaves. The wings and skeleton are blown away by the wind when the trap reopens. The whole process takes about ten days.

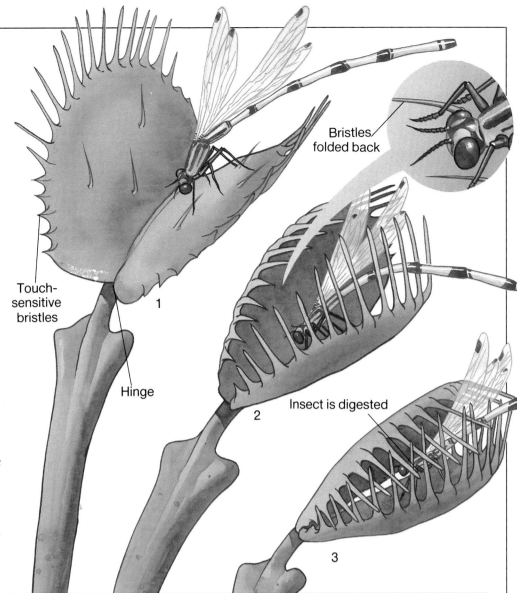

Bristles folded back

Touch-sensitive bristles

Hinge

Insect is digested

1

2

3

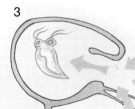

1

1. An animal touches the bladderwort's antennae which guide it towards the trap.

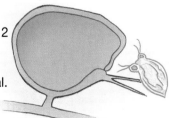

2

2. Trigger hairs are touched by the animal.

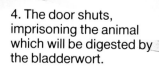

3

3. The door opens and the animal is sucked into the trap.

4. The door shuts, imprisoning the animal which will be digested by the bladderwort.

## UNDERWATER TRAPS

*The bladderwort is a plant that often grows in pondwater. Along its underwater stems are found tiny traps, called bladders, in which minute swimming creatures are caught. The smallest bladders are only 0.25 millimetres (.01 inches) wide, but some species of bladderwort can catch small fish in their traps.*

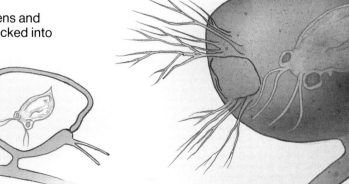

# Plants in water

Plants that live in salt or fresh water all face similar problems. Their leaves must float on or near the surface of the water in order to receive enough sunlight for photosynthesis. They must avoid getting waterlogged and sinking. In the sea and along the seashore, plants have the added problem of the drying effects of salt. Truly aquatic plants are known as hydrophytes. They have evolved various adaptations for their survival in water.

**THE WORLD OF WATER LILIES**
Water is much more buoyant (easier to float in) than air, but water plants still need to make sure that their leaves and shoots can reach the light for photosynthesis.

Water plants are largely supported by the water. This means that they do not need rigid stems to hold them upright as land plants do. Water lily stems are flexible and filled with air to keep them buoyant so that they can hold their leaves up to the light. The stems' flexibility allows them to adjust quickly to any changes in the water level.

Water lily roots grow down into the mud at the bottom of the water. They anchor the plant but are not used to take up minerals. Instead, minerals are absorbed all over the plant. As a result, water plants have reduced xylem and phloem systems compared to those of land plants. The spaces in the plant's **aerenchyma** allow air to circulate around the plant and to reach the roots.

Water lily leaves, or pads, float on the surface of the water. They have a tough, waxy epidermis so that water runs off them and they do not become waterlogged.

Water plants produce their flowers above water so that they can be pollinated by insects and by the wind. Water lily flowers open around midday to attract insects. They close again at dusk.

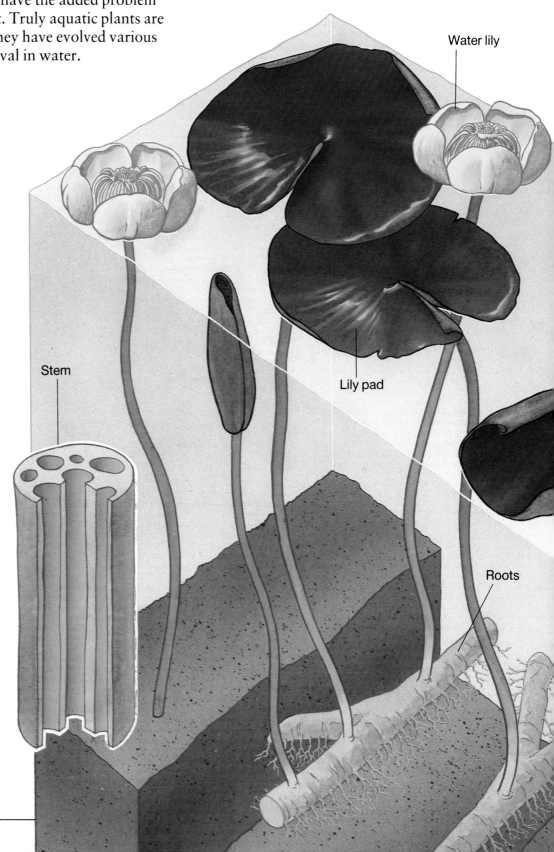

Water lily

Stem

Lily pad

Roots

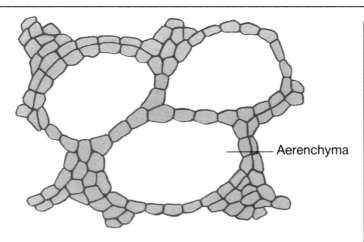

Aerenchyma

Water lily seeds are designed to float away from the parent plant. They have layers of air trapped inside their outer coats.

To stay afloat, aquatic plants contain structures like honeycombs. These are called aerenchyma. They consist of groups of cells with large, air-filled spaces in-between.

*As they photosynthesize, water plants release oxygen into the surrounding water. This is used by plants and animals for respiration.*

Seed

## SEAWEEDS
*Seaweeds are types of algae, with no true leaves, stems, roots or flowers. To avoid being swept out to sea, many anchor themselves to the rocks with a sucker-like holdfast. Some also have air-filled poppers, or 'bladders', on their fronds to keep them afloat as the sea washes in and out.*

## SALT SURVIVAL
*Plants that live along the seashore have to cope with high levels of salt in the spray coming from the sea. If salt lands on a plant's leaves it draws water out of them by osmosis, and dries them up. To prevent this, plants such as glassworts have developed fleshy leaves which contain large amounts of water.*

These plants also have a lower osmotic pressure in their cells than does the seawater surrounding them. This means that the normal balance is restored and the plants are able to draw in water from the surrounding environment. They also develop other measures to prevent water loss, such as having small leaves.

## WATER PLANT FACTS
*The giant Amazonian water lily has pads over six feet wide. They are buoyed up by air-filled ribs on their undersides.*

*The seeds of some water plants give off a glue-like substance. This makes the seeds stick to the bodies of water birds, and helps with their dispersal.*

*The fastest-growing plant is the Pacific giant kelp, a type of seaweed. It can grow 17 inches a day. However, it stops growing when it reaches a length of 215 feet.*

## ABOVE AND BELOW
Many water plants have two types of leaves. Above the surface broad leaves are used for collecting sunlight. The leaves below the surface are often feathery. This helps them to exchange gases during photo-synthesis and respiration.

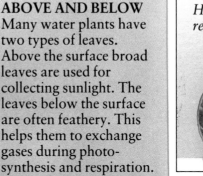

# Mystery fungi

There are about 80,000 species of fungi, ranging from molds and mildews to mushrooms and toadstools. Fungi are such peculiar organisms that botanists do not consider them to be plants at all. They have no flowers, leaves, true roots or stems. They do not contain chlorophyll so they cannot make their own food. Instead, they feed on living or dead matter. Fungi reproduce with tiny speck-like **spores** instead of seeds. Most of a fungus lies hidden underground, or inside tree trunks or other plants.

## FUNGUS FORMATION
The cap and stalk form the fruiting body of the mushroom. Its job is to make and scatter the spores.

A mushroom's spores grow on ridges, called gills, under the cap. The gills face downwards so that the spores can fall out and be scattered by the wind.

Cap

Gills

The cap protects the spores from the rain.

The stalk holds the cap up so that the falling spores can float away on the wind.

Stalk

Spores are produced in huge amounts, by cell division. Each spore will grow into an organism identical to its parent – if it lands in a suitable place.

Fungi are made up of a mass of tangled feeding threads, called hyphae. They spread over the fungi's food and suck out the goodness. A hypha has a cell wall but it is usually made of a substance called chitin, rather than the cellulose that forms plant cell walls. There is a vacuole and a lining of cytoplasm which may contain several small nuclei. The hypha does not contain any chloroplasts or chlorophyll.

The mesh of hyphae is called the mycelium.

Mycelium

## FOCUS ON MOLD

Molds grow very quickly on rotting bread or fruit. Their hyphae produce enzymes which turn the food into liquid. This liquid is then absorbed by the hyphae. The hyphae are easy to see as white or grey threads. Their tiny black tips, or sporangia, contain many thousands of spores.

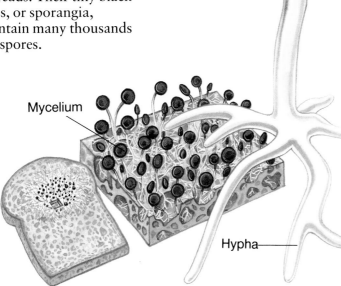

Sporangia

Mycelium

Hypha

The bread mold's mycelium covers the surface of the bread. Some hyphae grow upwards and their tips swell to form sporangia. Inside, the hyphae's protoplasm breaks down to form spores. The sporangia burst to release their spores.

Fungi that feed on dead or decaying matter are called **saprophytes**. They play an important part in breaking down dead leaves and wood and recycling their nutrients into the soil.

## FUNGI FACTS

*Some fungi are deadly poisonous. The death cap can kill a person in as little as six hours.*

*The fruiting bodies of giant puffballs can measure almost seven feet in circumference. As their name suggests, these fungi 'puff' their spores out in huge clouds. They do not have gills.*

*An ordinary edible mushroom can produce 30 million spores an hour.*

*Some fungi are very useful. Yeast is used in baking and brewing. The antibiotic drug, penicillin, comes from penicillium mold.*

*The study of fungi is called mycology.*

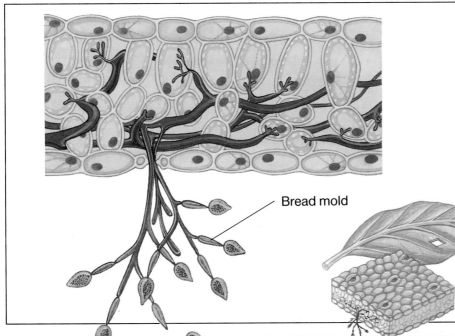

Bread mold

## FUNGUS PARASITES

*Fungi which feed on living plants or animals are called parasites. Their hyphae penetrate plant cells by producing an enzyme which breaks down the cellulose cell walls. Then the hyphae digest and absorb the contents of the cells. Many trees and plants are killed by fungi eating away at them.*

*To release their spores, the hyphae grow out of the stomata in the plants' leaves.*

# Glossary

**aerenchyma** the honeycomb-like structures found in aquatic plants that allow them to float in water.

**algae (singular, alga)** the simplest plants with bodies but no roots, stems or leaves.

**anther** the part of the male reproductive organ of a flower (the stamen) that contains the pollen sacs.

**anthocyanins** a group of pigments dissolved into a plant's cell sap that range from pink to purple.

**auxin** a special chemical that affects the growth of cells in response to the direction of light, the force of gravity, etc.

**bark** the outer layer of a woody stem such as a tree, made up of layers of dead cells.

**cambium** the region of cell division in a plant stem or root. In vascular bundles the cambium cells divide to make new xylem and phloem.

**carnivorous** describes an animal or plant that eats other animals.

**carotenoids** a group of pigments found in a plant's chromoplasts that range from yellow to red.

**carpel** the female reproductive part of a plant containing the stigma, style and ovary.

**cell** the microscopic building blocks that make up all living things.

**cell membrane** the thin skin that encloses the nucleus and cytoplasm inside a cell.

**cellulose** the tough, fibrous material found in plant cell walls. It is made up of glucose molecules.

**chlorophyll** a green pigment found in the chloroplasts of plant cells that absorbs the energy from sunlight for use in photosynthesis.

**chloroplasts** tiny organelles in the cytoplasm of a plant cell that trap sunlight needed for photosynthesis.

**chromoplasts** plastids in a plant's cytoplasm that contain certain pigments.

**cotyledons** the leaves contained inside a seed that feed the embryo as it starts to grow.

**cytoplasm** all the living material inside a cell except for the nucleus and vacuoles.

**deciduous** describes a plant that regularly sheds its leaves.

**dicotyledon** a plant with two seed leaves.

**enzymes** chemicals made by the cell that speed up the rate of chemical reactions inside the cell.

**epidermis** the single layer of cells that grows like a skin over a plant.

**evergreen** describes a plant that keeps its leaves all year round.

**fertilization** the process by which a male sex cell and a female sex cell meet, or fuse, forming a cell that develops into a new plant.

**flaccid** describes a plant cell that is wilting because of lack of water; flaccid cells give no support to a plant and it becomes limp.

**food chain** the sequence of events that starts with a plant being eaten by a herbivore, then a carnivore eating the herbivore, etc. However long the food chain becomes, it can be seen that all animals ultimately depend upon plants for food.

**fruit** a developed ovary. Many fruits, such as plums or cucumbers, are edible.

**fungus (plural fungi)** an organism that has no leaves, flowers, true roots or stems. Fungi cannot photosynthesize but feed off living or dead matter.

**glucose** a type of sugar that is used by cells for energy.

**heartwood** the dead, woody vessels in the center of a tree.

**lenticels** tiny holes in the bark of a tree that allow gases in and out for respiration.

**lignin** a strong, hard substance that builds up in the cell walls of xylem and forms a woody barrier, causing the xylem to die.

**membrane** a thin barrier through which certain substances can pass.

**meristems** the areas of a plant where cells divide rapidly and growth takes place.

**mesophyll** the name given to the palisade and spongy layers of a leaf.

**micropyle** the tiny hole in the ovule through which the pollen tube enters during fertilization.

**monocotyledon** a plant producing seeds with one seed leaf.

**mycelium** the mesh of feeding threads, or hyphae, that a fungus

spreads over its food.

**nectar** a sugary solution produced by flowers in the nectaries. It is an important source of food for insects.

**nucleus (plural nuclei)** the control center of the cell. Every cell contains at least one nucleus.

**organelle** a small structure in a plant's cytoplasm. Different types have different functions.

**osmosis** the movement of water molecules through a membrane from a weak to a strong solution.

**ovary** the female reproductive organ in a plant, containing one or more ovules. After fertilization the ovary will become the fruit.

**ovule** the female sex cell, contained inside the ovary. After fertilization the ovule will become a seed.

**palisade cells** the tall, column-shaped cells that lie just beneath the epidermis layer of a plant's leaves.

**phloem** the tubes that carry food from the leaves to the rest of the plant.

**photosynthesis** the process by which green plants make food from carbon dioxide and water, using energy from sunlight which is absorbed by their chlorophyll.

**pigment** a chemical which has a color, for example, chlorophyll is a green pigment.

**plastid** one of the types of organelles found in a plant's cytoplasm, for example chloroplasts and chromoplasts.

**plumule** the first shoot that grows from a seed.

**pollen** the male sex cell contained inside pollen sacs in the anther.

**pollination** the transfer of pollen from the anthers to the stigma. Pollen grains may be blown by the wind or carried by insects for pollination to occur.

**protoplasm** all the living matter in a cell, including the cytoplasm and nucleus.

**radicle** the first root that grows from a seed.

**respiration** the process that takes place inside all living cells by which energy is produced from food.

**sap** a syrupy solution containing

# Index

sugars made in the plant's leaves.

**saprophyte** an organism that feeds on dead or decaying matter.

**sapwood** the younger, outer layer of a woody stem.

**species** a group of organisms that resemble each other and can breed with each other.

**spore** a reproductive body produced by fungi and some simple plants.

**stamen** the male reproductive parts of a flower, made up of the filament and anther.

**starch** the form in which plants store excess food. A starch molecule is made up of hundreds of molecules of glucose.

**stigma** the tip of the carpel. It has a sticky surface so that pollen grains will stick to it.

**stomata (singular, stoma)** tiny holes, usually on the underside of a leaf, that open to allow carbon dioxide, oxygen and water vapor in and out of the leaf.

**transpiration** the evaporation of water through the stomata on the leaves of plants.

**transpiration stream** the process by which water is taken in through the roots of a plant, drawn up through the xylem tubes, and evaporates through the leaves.

**tropism** a change in direction or rate of growth by a plant in response to its environment.

**turgor** the pressure that keeps a plant cell fully extended and maintains a plant's shape.

**ultraviolet (UV) light** light that is not visible to the human eye but which is produced in large amounts by the sun.

**vacuoles** the large, fluid-filled spaces inside plant cells.

**vascular bundle** the compact arrangement of xylem and phloem found in most plant stems.

**vascular tissue** the system of narrow tubes inside a plant, carrying water, minerals and food, made up of xylem and phloem.

**xylem** tubes that carry water and minerals up from the roots through the plant to the leaves.

abscission layer 28
adventitious roots 23
aerenchyma 40, 41
algae 9, 14, 16, 41
anther 25, 30, 35
anthocyanins 26, 27, 28
apex (leaf point) 10
aquatic plants 39, 40–1
auxins 22, 36, 37, 38

bark 18, 20–1
bladderwort 39
buds 24, 29, 35

cacti 13
cambium 16, 17, 18, 19, 20
carnivorous plants 38, 39
carotenoids 26, 27, 28
carpel 24, 30
cell division 8, 9, 16, 20, 22, 34, 42
cell structure 8–9
cellulose 8, 9, 23
chitin 42
*Chlamydomonas* 8, 9, 14
chlorophyll 9, 11, 14, 15, 27, 28, 35
chloroplasts 9, 10, 11, 14, 15
chromoplasts 26
climbing plants 38
color 24, 26–7, 28
conifers 13, 29, 33
cortex 16
cotyledons 33, 34
cytoplasm 8, 9, 11, 13, 42

day-neutral plants 37
deciduous trees 13, 28
diatoms 8, 9
dicotyledons 33

endosperm 33
enzymes 15, 34, 39, 43
epidermis 10, 11, 16, 40
evergreen trees 29

fertilization 30–1, 32, 33
fibrous roots 23
flowers 24–5, 26, 31, 35, 37, 40
food, storage of 15, 19
fruit 31, 32, 33
fungi 16, 42–3

gametes 31
generative nucleus 30, 31
geotropism 36
germination 34–5, 37
girdle scar 29
glucose 14, 15, 23, 34
grana 15
gravity 22, 36

growth 34–5, 36
guard cells 8, 9, 11, 12

haptotropism 38
heartwood 19
hilum 33
Hooke, Robert 20
hydrophytes 40
hydrotropism 36
hyphae 42, 43

lamina 10
leaves 10–11, 12, 13, 14, 16, 23, 28–9, 35, 40
lenticels 21
lignin 17, 19
long-day plants 37
lupin 24, 25, 34

medullary rays 19
membrane 8, 9, 15
mesophyll 11
micropyle 31, 33, 34
monocotyledons 33
mosses 16
molds 43
mycelium 42, 43
mycology 43

nectar 24
nuclei 8, 9, 30, 31, 42

orchids 23, 24, 26, 33
organelles 8, 9
osmosis 12, 13, 23, 34, 36, 41
ovary 24, 31, 32, 33
ovule 24, 30, 31, 32, 33

palisade cells 8, 9, 11, 14
parasitic plants 17, 43
penicillin 43
petals 24, 35, 37
petiole 10
phloem 8–9, 10, 14, 16, 17, 18, 19, 23, 34, 40
photoperiodism 37
photosynthesis 10, 11, 12, 14–15, 22, 27, 28, 35, 40, 41
phototropism 36
phytochrome 37
pigments 9, 11, 14, 15, 26, 27, 28
piliferous layer 22, 23
plastids 9, 26
plumule 33, 34, 35
pods 32
pollen 24, 25, 30–31
pollen sacs 25, 30
pollination 24, 25, 26, 30–1, 37, 40

protopolasm 9, 43

quantasomes 15
quinine 21

radicle 33, 34
receptacle 24
respiration 10, 12, 14, 21, 41
root hairs 23, 34
roots 12, 13, 17, 22–3, 34, 36, 40

sap 9, 12, 14, 16, 17, 26
saprophytes 43
sapwood 19
scent 24, 27
seaweed 27, 41
seeds 31, 32–3, 34, 37, 41
sensitivity 36–9
sepals 24, 35
sex cells 24, 25, 30, 31
short-day plants 37
sieve tubes 17
single-celled plants 8, 9
sporangia 43
spores 42, 43
stamens 25, 30
starch 15, 36
stems 16, 18, 40
stigma 24, 25, 30, 31, 35
stomata 9, 11, 12–13, 15, 43
suberin 20

tap roots 23
tepals 24
testa 33
translocation 17
transpiration 10, 12, 13, 28
tree rings 19
trees 8, 13, 16, 18–19, 20, 21, 28, 29, 33
tropisms 36, 38
tube nucleus 30
turgor 13, 37

vacuoles 9, 13, 22, 36, 42
vascular bundles 16, 17, 18, 29
vascular tissue 10, 16, 18
Venus fly-trap 39
violanin 27

water lily 40–1
wilting 13, 38
wood 16, 18–19

xylem 10, 12, 13, 16, 17, 18, 19, 23, 40

yeast 43

zone of elongation 22
zygote 31